The Semiotics of the
Built Environment

ADVANCES IN SEMIOTICS
Thomas A. Sebeok, General Editor

The Semiotics of the Built Environment

An Introduction to Architectonic Analysis

Donald Preziosi

INDIANA UNIVERSITY PRESS
Bloomington

Manufactured in the United States of America

Library of Congress Cataloging in Publication Data
Preziosi, Donald, 1941-
    The semiotics of the built environment.

    (Advances in semiotics)
    Bibliography: p. 111
    1. Signs and symbols in architecture. 2. Semiotics. I. Title. II. Series.
NA2500.P74   720'.1   78-20404
ISBN 0-253-17638-7

2 3 4 5 6 7 85 84 83 82 81

For my Parents and Grandparents

Contents

Preface

This book is concerned with the analysis and description of the built environment as a semiotic system—as a system of meaningful signs. It seeks to establish some of the principal ways in which what will be termed *architectonic systems* are similar to and different from other forms of human symbolic communication.

As an introduction to the systematic analysis of built environments from a semiotic perspective, the present volume is intended to be relatively self-contained, presupposing little or no familiarity with the subject on the part of the reader. At the same time, the reader familiar with current research and speculation in semiotics, anthropology and art and architectural history will find many contemporary issues and problems addressed both directly and indirectly.

The present text is an arrested moment in an ongoing research project begun in 1970 while I was teaching at Yale, continuing since 1973 at MIT. During this time, the research has been supported in part by various grants and fellowships, including a Fellowship from the National Endowment for the Humanities (1973), the Wenner-Gren Foundation for Anthropological Research (1975, Summer), and various supportive grants from the Department of the History of Art at Yale. I am grateful also for the in-house leaves from the Department of Art and Architecture at MIT during 1973 and 1974 which enabled me to put in order the accumulation of data begun several years before. Initial field work for the analysis of the specific data employed in the present text was supported by a Charles Eliot Norton Fellowship from Harvard, and a Harvard Travelling Fellowship (1964-66).

The number of persons whose interactions with the writer have affected the present study to its benefit is very great. Many colleagues, students and friends have left their imprint on this book in direct and indirect ways, and it has been often the case that a chance remark or a brief conversation in a hallway or convention lobby has stimulated a train of thought which ultimately led to the clarification of the aims of this project.

I must above all acknowledge the contributions of many students and friends in my graduate seminars at Yale and MIT whose lively, informed and insightful conversations and enormous energies were crucial both in the launching of this project and in its continuation. My teachers at Harvard and my colleagues at Yale, MIT and Cornell have similarly been generous with their time with someone perhaps obsessively impatient to define the right questions to ask. The following list is partial, and I have tried to include all those with whom some (even momentary) personal interaction has affected the present report to its benefit: Wayne Andersen, Stanford Anderson, Michael Bales, Keith Basso, Dwight Bolinger, Marie-Henriette Carre, Whitney Chadwick, Kwang-chih Chang, William Davenport, Peter Eisenmann, Robin Fawcett, Mario Gandelsonas, Marie-Christine Gangneux, Paul Garvin, Charles Gates, Wladimir Godzich, Ernst Gombrich, Steven Grossberg, François Guerin, Morris Halle, M.A.K. Halliday, Dolores Hayden, Elmar Holenstein, Roman Jakobson, Hong-bin Kang, Karl Lamberg-Karlovsky, George Kubler, Sydney Lamb, Heather Lechtman, Neil Levine, Shelagh Lindsey, Robert Manoff, Miranda Marvin, Jonathan

Matthews, Arden and Ulric Neisser, Sheldon Nodelman, Christian Norberg-Schulz, Werner Oechslin, Maggie Rogow, Irving Rouse, Lynne Rutkin, Nicholas Rykwert, Meyer Schapiro, Hal Scheffler, Vincent Scully, Jr., Thomas Sebeok, Grace Seiberling, Edward Stankiewicz, Arthur Steinberg, Eléanor Steindler, Linda Suter, Alexander Tzonis, Paolo Valesio, Dora Vallier, and Linda Waugh. I would also like to thank the patient owners of the Piroschke Cafe in Cambridge, where this book was begun. I am most particularly grateful to Linda Waugh and Roman Jakobson, whose continuing stimulation and support have clarified the direction of my questions.

*   *   *   *

As an attempt at a systematic analysis, the present volume introduces some special terminology. An attempt has been made to keep this to a minimum, and to provide a running explanation of potentially unfamiliar terms. The book includes a glossary of new or unusual terms, cross-indexed to first occurrences in the text by means of a superscript letter (thus, *architectonic*[a]). Plates I-VIII, Chapter II, were drawn by David Peck, and the text was patiently and expertly typed and composed by Mrs. Coraleen L. Rooney.

Cambridge, Mass.; Peacham, Vermont; Ithaca, N.Y.; New Haven, Conn.

The Semiotics of the
Built Environment

Marco Polo describes a bridge, stone by stone.
    'But which is the stone that supports the bridge?'
Kublai Khan asks.
    'The bridge is not supported by one stone or another,'
Marco answers, 'but by the line of the arch that they form.'
    Kublai Khan remains silent, reflecting. Then he adds:
'Why do you speak to me of the stones? It is only the arch that matters to me.'
    Polo answers: 'Without stones there is no arch.'

                (Italo Calvino, *Invisible Cities*, 1972, p. 82)

Much of the motivation for extending structural analysis beyond language, from the standpoint of linguistics, is not to assimilate the rest of culture to language, but to discover more precisely the place of language.

           Dell Hymes, Proceedings of the Colloque Internationale du C.N.R.S., *L'emploi des calculateurs en archéologie, problèmes sémiologiques et mathématiques*, Marseilles, April 1969

Chapter I
Introduction

Humans live in an extraordinarily complex world of made objects. In any given environmental setting, the array of copresent objects exist as components in a variety of interrelated sign systems, each system addressed to partly unique and partly redundant functions. It is characteristically the case that the same object formation will have variant meanings and behavioral associations in different contexts, or even in the same context at different times. Moreover, both object formations and their conceptual associations change over time, often in different ways.

It is a major problem of human knowledge to understand how such complexities arise and how it is we come to scaffold our individual and collaborative lives through the appropriation of and interaction with this omnipresent world of objects.

Not only do we use and make objects; objects in turn have, in a sense, made us what we have become as a species. It seems evident that we have evolved ourselves in large part to interact with this artifactual[a] world of sign-formations—in other words, that human evolution is in part the product of our long interaction with systems of built forms.[1]

Like verbal language, the *built environment*[a]—what will be called here the *architectonic*[a] *code* —is a panhuman phenomenon. No human society exists without artifactually reordering its environment—without employing environmental formations (whether made or appropriated) as sign-tokens in a system of visual communication, representation and expression.

Every human society communicates architectonically. The component units of an architectonic code[a] or system[a] consist of contrastively-opposed formations in media addressed to visual perception. Distinctions or disjunctions in material formation are intended to cue culture-specific differences in meaning in a manner precisely analogous to other semiotic systems such as verbal language or bodily gesturing.

In the broadest sense, communication consists of the transmission of information regarding the perception of similarities and differences. The system of the built environment, like any semiotic[a] code, is a complexly-ordered device for the cueing of such perceptions.

This does not mean that every single disjunction in material formation perceptually palpable to a given observer or analyst will necessarily be directly correlated to differences in meaning.

1

In other words, every architectonic code specifies which disjunctions in formation are to be correlated to differences in meaning. Not everything in a built environment is meaningful in quite the same way. Some differences may be trivial, irrelevant, and normally overlooked by the code, while others, seemingly minute to an outsider, will often be profoundly significant to the native user of a given built environment. A difference between crimson and scarlet in the color of houses in one code may be seen as contextual variants[a] of a single color-scheme, while in another code the color-contrast is strongly linked to differences in social status, and so forth.

An architectonic system, as a system of signs, is hierarchically organized. A given architectonic formation such as a building is composed of material units of different sizes, shapes, weights, etc.; each component entity serves a given systemic function in the organization of the whole. But paradoxically, an architectonic code is not organized like the material-aggregation of a house, in an 'atomistic' fashion. Rather, like any semiotic system, the system of the built environment is best seen, to paraphrase Heisenberg,[2] as

> a complicated tissue of events in which connections of different kinds alternate or overlap or combine and thereby determine the texture of the whole.

The architectonic code is essentially a *system of relationships* in which significative entities are defined in terms of their relative positions in a multidimensional network of relationships. For this reason, two apparently identical formations in different systems are only superficially 'homonymous,' since each belongs to, and is defined principally in relation to, the overall system of signs of which each is an exemplar or material realization.

A simple analogy may be made with colors. The perception of a given color is in large part a function of the environment in which that color is embedded; hence a given grey seen against a darker ground will appear lighter than the same grey seen against a lighter ground. In a similar fashion, the object-formations in a given environmental setting (a given architectonic corpus of forms) will acquire different significations depending upon its *systemic*[a] relationships with other copresent formations. Any architectonic object is perceptually and conceptually different in contrastive contexts. Two 'identical' Hilton hotels in Prague and Casablanca are not the same architectonic formations.

In the broadest sense, the task of architectonic analysis involves the elaboration of models to account for the invariance and variability of object formations in given built environments. The architectonic code is built upon a principle of *relational invariance*[a], as is any semiotic system. Its 'vocabulary' is spatial and geometric in nature, and architectonic formations are organized according to the parameters of topological, perspective and euclidean metric formative features.

As we shall see below, this does *not* mean that what distinguishes an architectonic system from other systems are characteristically 'regularized' geometric constructs: the gardens of Versailles are not any more 'architectonic' than the ephemeral encampments in an appropriated environment by !Kung Bushmen or Australian aborigines who frequently do not 'build' in our sense of the term.[3]

Architectonic analysis begins by posing simple questions such as "what is similar and what is different about two formations," and goes on to establish the many complex relationships among objects in an environmental array, so as to formulate generic models which account for formative variation and invariance.

But the object of architectonic study is not only formative variation *per se*, but rather the relationships between formal variation and variations in meaning and reference. In other words, the objects of analytic study are sign-formations or significative unities and their cross-indexed networks of relationships. An architectonic *sign*[a] is a combination of a formation (that-which-signifies) and a meaning (that-which-is-signified). A system or code of sign-formations is an ordered body of rules which specify the conventional associations between formations and meanings, and between the signs (as combinations of formations and meanings) themselves and other signs, of the same or of different types.

But 'meaning' is not, strictly speaking, a thing in itself; it comprises specified sets of relationships among formations both within a system and external to that system. Furthermore, this is not to be confused with 'external reference' in the sense of association to something non-semiotic or existing with some ontological reality outside of human perception and cognition. In this respect we shall follow Peirce's formulation of meaning as the translation of one sign into another,[4] whether the latter is a component member of the same sign-system[a] or another sign-system. A culture, in the broadest sense, consists of time-and-space-specific sets of rules of correlation among sign-systems.[5]

As a system of signs, a built environment does not exist in a vacuum but is co-occurrent with ensembles of other sign systems in different media. Each sign system offers certain advantages over others under the varying conditions of daily life. A built environment does certain things which verbal language does not do, or only does by weak approximation and circumlocution—and vice-versa.

Sign systems often provide partially-redundant ways of doing functionally-equivalent things. I can maintain my privacy, for example, by building a wall around myself, putting up a 'no trespassing' sign, wearing a loincloth, or gesturing dramatically whenever a stranger comes within six meters of my person.

But normally, humans will do several things at the same time, and will orchestrate anything at their disposal to communicate information. Architectonic formations, in daily life, are embedded in large-scale *communicative events*[a], which incorporate a great many different kinds of signs in various media, simultaneously and in tandem, in syntagmatic and paradigmatic association.[6]

What distinguishes us as a species is not the possession and use of any one powerful method of communication—verbal language, artifacts, etc.,—but rather a tendency to employ anything and everything in a communicative fashion, to use any available resources in a significant manner, to transform anything into a sign. While we are far from being able to reconstruct in an unambiguous manner the picture of human origins, it does seem clear that the origins of language, somatic gesturing, and environmental structuring are inextricably interwoven and mutually implicative.[7] Each of the sign systems evolved by humans is (relatively) coherent in its own right, but at the same time each is *designed* to operate in concert with others, and each incorporates elements which are functionally cross-indexed with signs in other systems.[8] In other words, each sign system incorporates sign-formations which are semantically ambiguous without reference to signs in other systems.

The architectonic code is one of several fundamental panhuman sign-systems which in concert provide individuals and groups with a multimodal[a] and multiply-stereoscopic template for the creation of humanly-meaningful realities. No one sign-system creates the human world in itself. No single perspective is complete in itself. Rather, each contributes its partly-unique perspective on the totalities of sociocultural experience.

In the writer's view it is fair to say that our understanding of the built environment is in certain respects still in its adolescence. We know both so little and so much about this extraordinary human phenomenon, rivalled in its encyclopedic power only by verbal language itself.

In effect, our understanding of the built environment still has the form of the component images of a teleidoscope which focuses upon an object and refracts its image into random sections, each section coveted by domains of several different analytic disciplines. A science of 'architectonics'[a] exists only as the sum of phantom images in the work of a great many students of different aspects of the built environment.

The emergence of an architectonics as an integrated framework for the study of built environments has become an inevitable and necessary result of the ongoing overlapping and convergence of many different perspectives on environmental structuration. But it cannot come about as a simple sum of the aforementioned phantom images, for these do not add up to a coherent domain, and many of their perspectives, methods and conclusions are mutually contradictory. 'Architectonics' should be more than an academic cover-term for superimposed and mutually indigestible disciplines. Research and methods elaborated under the rubrics of proxemics, kinesics, environmental psychology, man-environment relations, architectural history, body-language, and perceptual psychology all have significant input into architectonics, but not all of what each of these has to say will be relevant. Moreover, each of these approaches has been elaborated for different ends: they are not all component bricks adding up to a structurally-integrated edifice, however cleverly we pile them on top of each other.

One of the primary aims of the present study is to design a coherent framework for architectonic analysis. This book has both the merits and faults of any first approximation, as will become evident to the reader. It is in certain respects both too specific and too general. But this is a necessary concomitant of an attempt to clear the air (or the jungle), for a great many things need to be addressed—some very general received assumptions as well, as a great many analytic details concerned with methodological specifics. If first approximations are like midwives, then the present study aims to ease delivery by setting a reasonable stage. Moreover, this text appears in print at a time when the research which led to the preparation of this manuscript has advanced beyond the discussions here by over a year. A number of issues addressed here have received a different focus in subsequent writings, notably the crucial problem of metaphorical and metonymic relations in architectonic signing (see Appendix A).

The are many reasons for our inability to adequately handle the complex systematicity[a] of the built environment. In part this inability is related to a lack of adequately lucid methodological frameworks. It is at the same time related to our subscription to many assumptions—hidden and patent—in the received tradition.

Among students of built environments, there is very little agreement on many fundamental issues, including the nature of the medium itself, the basic units of organization, the meanings and functions of architectonic objects, and the relationships of built environments with other symbol systems. Moreover, the task of architectonic analysis has for many generations been a captive either of art-historical connoisseurship and 'criticism' directed at the social and 'aesthetic' merits of formations, or of architectural 'analysis' aimed at sharpening the wits of would-be practitioners. Architectonic descriptive theory has often been the servant of prescriptive[a] ideologizing. What has passed for architectural theory has commonly consisted of little more than semantic maneuvering to gain a maximal congruence of idiosyncratic classification in the service of academic and professional ambition, and architectural theory has tended to be a fragile ship open to the cross-currents of fashion.

But to question whether 'architecture' is 'art,' craft, engineering (physical or social), theatre, housing, or three-dimensional economics is as pointless as asking the same of language. We shall explore this pointless but crucial issue below. For the moment it will be sufficient to sensitize ourselves to the *multifunctionality*[a] of architectonic formations.[9]

Moreover, as will be evident below, we shall attempt to show that it is only through a *semiotic* framework that the complex multifunctionality of the built environment can be adequately situated, and its relationship with other aspects of culture more clearly oriented.

A great deal of confusion has centered upon the nature of the architectonic *medium* itself. In contrast, for example, with the linguistic code, which employs a relatively uniform and narrowly circumscribed medium of acoustic signals addressed to the vocal-auditory channel—and which, it now seems evident, is processed by the brain differently from nonlinguistic acoustic phenomena,[10]—the medium of the built environment can be anything from frozen blocks of water in the Arctic to carved limestone and poured concrete, from bamboo and mud and animal skins to clearings of a forest floor or the appropriated flora of a given landscape.

But this confusion is more apparent than real. The medium of the built environment is in fact anything and everything visually-palpable which can be employed to serve place-making functions. As a system of relationships, the architectonic code signifies conceptual associations through similarities and differences in visually-palpable formation *per se*. It is important to distinguish contextual variation in material realization from the geometric properties of formations themselves. It is the latter which constitute the 'vocabulary' of architectonic formations, as we shall see.

The physical medium of the built environment, then, is potentially coterminous with the entire range of material resources of the planetary biosphere which can be employed to construct significative formations addressed to the visual channel[a]. The architectonic system of a given culture employs anything at hand which it perceives as suitable for communicating architectonically.

This is not to say, however, that everything so palpable is, in a given culture, a necessary component of an architectonic code. A room, a sewing machine in the corner of that room, and a tree or mountain seen through the window of that room—however else the latter three may function—may serve as signs in a system of signs creating a conceptual world. Each of these 'natural' or man-made formations may acquire architectonic significance by virtue of their space-shaping and space-defining properties, as these are differentially appropriated by different cultures.

Moreover, what is significant in one architectonic system may be differently significant or nonrelevant in another system. Once again it is necessary to stress the fact that the significance of given formations is in large measure a function of definition by a system as a whole.

A necessary question arises as to where we are to fix the boundaries or limits of an architectonic system. The answer is again in concert with the foregoing remarks—anything visually-palpable *may* be incorporated into an architectonic code by virtue of its palpable space-defining properties; but what in fact is so employed will be a function of a given culture-specific system.

It will be evident, then, that while an architectonic system includes what in Western parlance is termed 'architecture,'—namely 'buildings' and their infrastructures[a]—it will necessarily also incorporate everything up to and including the generic 'environment' itself. And in some societies the mountain on the horizon is assimilated to the system of the built world, while in others it may be seen as an irregularity in the 'empty' space between cities—although even in the latter case, its significance is necessarily architectonic.

A corollary of this is the fact that an architectonic code is not necessarily equivalent to the sum of *artifactual* or made formations, but will normally incorporate formations 'appropriated' from a 'natural' landscape. In other words, an architectonic system can get along without 'buildings.'

Such a situation is aptly characterized in the following observation:

> It takes the women only three-quarters of an hour to build their shelters, but half the time at least the women's whim is not to build shelters at all. In this case, they sometimes put up two sticks to symbolize the entrance of the shelters so that the family may orient itself as to which side is the man's side and which the woman's side of the fire. Sometimes they do not bother with the sticks.[11]

An important property of built environments is the dispensibility of formations. This is not a privileged property of !Kung Bushmen or of people living in warm climates, but is a property of any architectonic system. While it may be trivially obvious that one doesn't need to have a garage if one drives a car, it is nevertheless an observation which is the concomitant of two features of architectonic systems: first, a given environmental array need not incorporate every formation potential in a code (any more than a given sentence need not contain all the vocabulary of a language), and, secondly, form does not follow function any more than function follows form. In other words, in the second case there will, in any code, be alternative means for accomplishing isofunctional or equivalent ends. In the first case, it is evident that any given semiotic code unfolds piecemeal in space and time.

These properties are shared by the built environment with any semiotic system. It is therefore the case that even in certain 'traditional' societies which appear to 'have' no 'architecture', the given environment is itself employed architectonically, as has been observed by Rapoport and others.[12] A group of elders sitting in a circle in a meadow once a month is as fully 'architectonic' as a council chamber.

But if the latter observation is so, then it is important to be clear about the 'boundaries' of architectonic communication, representation and expression vis-à-vis other nonarchitectonic signings in the visual channel. We must distinguish between 'somatotopic'[a] behaviors wherein bodies construct spatial frameworks *architectonically*, and somatic gesturings wherein body-parts such as the limbs and portions of the face are employed in support of a verbal message. In the first case, a body or bodies serve space-defining functions partly surrogative of artifactual formations, whereas in the latter case kinetic formations composed by parts of a body are intended to communicate information in a manner analogous to or derivative of verbal language.

The latter will incorporate various kinds of 'sign' languages which serve as replacements for vocalizations or verbal messages. These may be of several types, depending upon the ability of a given gesture-system to more or less 'fully' replace linguistic signings: some systems are relatively autonomous of verbal language, while others may be closely cross-indexed with vocalizations and principally serve paralinguistic or augmentative functions relative to vocalizations. In the latter case would be included various kinds of gestural signals which operate in close rhythmic synchrony with speech.

Each kind of gestural sign-system is differently related to linguistic and architectonic signings, but it is evident that autonomous somatic sign-systems do exist independently of either. It now appears to have been demonstrated that in the absence of linguistic models, deaf children will spontaneously develop systems of 'sign' language which incorporate a number of salient design features shared with non-somatic sign-systems such as verbal language.[13]

It is evidently the case that both verbal language and the architectonic code are similarly 'ambitious' in their capacities to assimilate the world of experience to themselves in an encylcopedic fashion. That is to say, both manifest an analogous 'effability' in attempting to translate any content, including those codified by other systems, into their own symbol systems.[14]

It is equally clear that the differences between these two fundamental human modalities[a] are profound in a number of respects, and many of these differences are necessary products of their contrastive media.

One of the most striking aspects of architectonic codes induced by their formative media is a property of *object-permanence*. That is to say, architectonic formations manifest a permanence of 'broadcast' *relative to* other systems of signing such as verbal language and 'sign' language. An architectonic formation will continue to broadcast long after the more ephemeral transmissions of a speech act, whose traces remain in the auditory channel only momentarily. Thus any given architectonic formation may serve to 'contextualize' or 'ground' other kinds of semiotic formations, since its signal will 'decay' at a much slower rate rhan the latter.

But it is important *not* to take the property of object-permanence in an *absolute* sense: we are speaking of a permanence relative to other modalities. Moreover, there is a very wide range of permanence, even in the same corpus of forms. A formation may continue to 'broadcast' for generations, centuries or millenia, but it may also be a transitory and ephemeral phenomenon, such as an umbrella in a rainstorm, a place on a stage created by spotlights lasting for two hours, a parade down mainstreet, or a set of space-framing gestures by bodies. Furthermore, the relative permanence of architectonic signals is a joint product of the characteristics of certain signing materials and the intentions of builders. There is, furthermore, no direct correlation between the slowness of the rate of decay of formations or transmissions and cultural sophistication or even technological sophistication.

The ability of architectonic formations to 'contextualize' non-architectonic formations—a result of the parameters of its media—does *not* mean (as so often may be inferred in literature on linguistic signing) that the built environment is a kind of passive 'stage-set' for other semiotic behavior. The moon necessarily does revolve on its axis even though we normally see only one of its faces. A building can only best be understood in this regard as a sustained note in an ongoing and dynamic orchestration of signs in different media, some of which are more ephemeral than others in their sensory channels. While this is not always easy to see, particularly from the standpoint of a more 'monument'-oriented art-historical perspective, it is nevertheless an important property of architectonic systems, and has to be taken into account in any serious semiotic study.[15]

Parenthetically, another factor related to this, essentially a misconstrual of the consequences of this phenomenon, should be noted. It is simply not the case that we apprehend the complexities of a built environment only because of our abilities to linguistically label components of an environment. This is equivalent to saying that verbal formations are only meaningful because of their connections to external reference.[16] We will take up this question in some detail below in our discussion of architectonic meaning.

A built environment is an ongoing, dynamically unfolding array of signs, existing spatially and temporally. A given environmental setting reveals the existence of sign-formations of contrastive relative ages much in the same manner that a given sentence will reveal the copresence of formative elements with different histories. The same sentence (e.g., 'the cats jumped over the sheep (pl.)') may incorporate two different ways of forming plurals, one historically more recent than the other.

Built environments are dynamic in yet another sense. An architectonic formation is not necessarily stable or static, but may be rolled, floated or flown away, or carried in disassembled fashion on one's back to the site of the next encampment. Once again, formational permanence is relative.

Perhaps the most important confusion regarding the nature and organization of architectonic systems is concerned with the identification and definition of its organizational *units*, and it is to this question that much of the present study is directed. We will begin to address this problem in the next section.

It is becoming increasingly evident that our growing understanding of the built environment as a complex system of signs will have important ramifications for the study of other semiotic systems such as verbal language and somatic signing. It is clear that the latter do not exist in a vacuum, despite tendencies to study the latter in that manner. Our understanding of the internal organization of these other panhuman codes should be significantly affected by our picture of the organization of architectonic systems, in ways which at present can only be partially outlined.

These changes will be induced by an ongoing shift in analytic orientation from the formal mechanisms of linguistics to the characteristic embeddedness of linguistic (and other) signings in large-scale communicative events. In addition, as our understanding of the systematicities of various kinds of nonverbal communication expands, we shall be in a better position to understand the unique power and potential of each of the sign-systems employed by humans in the ongoing semiotic bricolage of sociocultural life.

FOOTNOTES

CHAPTER I

[1] See D. Preziosi, *The Origins of the Built World* (1978c), forthcoming, for a detailed discussion of this question.

[2] W. Heisenberg, *Physics and Philosophy*, New York, 1958, 107.

[3] See J. Yellen, *Archaeological approaches to the Present: Models for Reconstructing the Past*, New York, 1977, on the !Kung; and A. Rapoport, "Australian Aborigines and the Definition of Place," in *Man-Environment Systems*, January 1970.

[4] Charles Sanders Peirce, *Collected Writings* 4.127.

[5] See Preziosi, *op. cit.*, Chapter V, for a discussion of cultural organization as a relational system of sign-ensembles, summarized below in our concluding Chapter.

[6] Discussed in detail in D. Preziosi, 'Multimodal Communication,' (1978k), forthcoming; see Appendix below.

[7] See Preziosi, 1978c, Chapters IV and V.

[8] See above, n. 6.

[9] See Preziosi, 1978c, Chapter III, and *id.*, "Architectonic and Linguistic Signs," paper presented to the International Conference on the Semiotics of Art, Ann Arbor, Michigan, May 3-6, 1978, to be published.

[10] Evidence for this is discussed in R. Jakobson and L. R. Waugh, *The Sound Shape of Language*, Chapter I (Bloomington, Indiana, 1979, forthcoming). It remains to be seen if the perception of architectonic/*artifactual* formations is equivalently lateralized in the brain.

[11] L. Marshall, "!Kung Bushman Bands," *Africa*, vol. 30, no. 4, 1960, 342-3.

[12] See above, n. 3, and *id., House Form & Culture*, Englewood Cliffs, New Jersey, 1969.

[13] Reported by S. Goldin-Meadow and H. Feldman, "The Development of Language-Like Communication without a Language Model," *Science*, Vol. 197, 401-3, 22 July 1977. Relationships between sign-systems is discussed in Preziosi, 1978k, with reference to gesture.

[14] The question of 'effability' is insightfully discussed by U. Eco, *A Theory of Semiotics*, Bloomington, Indiana, 1976, 173, and in Preziosi, 1978e.

[15] There is an important *operational paradox* here, for sign-systems offer alternative perspectives on the contents of other systems such that each may serve to a certain extent as a 'metalanguage' with respect to others in sociocultural contexts. See Preziosi, 1978c, Chapter V, and *id.*, "Toward a Relational Theory of Culture," *The Third LACUS Forum*, Columbia, South Carolina, 1977, 278-288.

[16] On the question of referentiality, see M. Silverstein, "Shifters, Lexical Categories and Cultural Description, in K. Basso and H. Selby, eds., *Meaning in Anthropology*, Albuquerque, New Mexico, 1976, 11-56; and U. Eco, *op. cit.*, 58-66 and 163-171. The statement by Leach that "A modern urban street is wholly man-made and it is only because all the things in it carry individual names, i.e., symbolic labels, that we can recognize what they are," E. Leach, *Culture & Communication*, Cambridge, England, 1976, 33, is, on the face of it, untrue. See Preziosi, 1978c, Chapter V, and below, on architectonic meaning.

Chapter II
Formal Structure

I am sitting in a coffee shop in a university town. Through the window and across a narrow street I can see one of the facades of an old brick trolley-barn, several stories high. It has been many years since the electric trolleys came here at the end of their run, inched their ways up the central ramp to the storage bays on the upper floors, and passed the night. Recently, the building has been transformed into a multi-level shopping mall known as "The Garage."

In its external appearance, the facade of the building resembles an ancient Roman apartment block such as those known from the old port city of Ostia two millenia ago. There are resonances also, for the historically-minded, with Italian Renaissance palazzi, with several tiers of large, arched windows, articulated roof-mouldings, and the like.

This is most extraordinary.

Indeed, it is remarkably puzzling and delightful at the same time. Here is an object masquerading as an ancient block of flats, designed to serve as a barn for electric trolleys and now serving as a bazaar dispensing everything from cheesecake to "classic" science-fiction comic-books.

How can this be? What is being "communicated" (if anything) by this bizarre hybrid of forms and usages? What *were* the intentions of the structure's designer(s)—and how many ways are its messages variously read by users and passers-by in the course of a day? Are the connotations of this object's appearance variable from year to year, and across generations of students? What is its future? Indeed, is it at all possible to capture the intended and effective meanings of this remarkable object in any clear and coherent way, even at a random moment in time?

Not that the very place I am sitting in is any less remarkable. It is a large cubicle, a space-cell in a large building compound erected over the last decade, containing a large variety of space-cells, housing a bewildering variety of functions, some directly related to the administrative business of the university, others entirely independent.

The cubicle to the left is a hair salon. It is otherwise of the same general configuration and external facade-setting as my cafe: same glass doors, same brick flooring, same painted brick walls within a single bay of the poured-concrete structural frame. To the right is a shop selling over-priced clothing to unknowing Saturday shoppers, then a shoe store, and finally an art-supply shop.

In what might be fantasized as a relatively reasonable universe, would we expect that each of these "functions" might elicit different material or formal settings? And if so, why? To be sure, the infrastructural organization of these otherwise identical cubicles varies from shop to shop, "reflecting" in some (presently) conventional sense their variant purposes and internal routines. But why this or that infrastructure? If we move about more widely in the city, we will notice that there will be other stores selling otherwise identical wares amidst strikingly different settings.

It is by no means a trivial question to ask how and why this extraordinary state of affairs has come about. We take this situation so for granted that such a question hardly surfaces at all. Perhaps this is as it should be. Often, such a question emerges only when architectural rhetoricians claim some "innate" connection between the formal structures they are proposing and its intended programme or usage: Ledoux's hall for the sexual initiation of adolescents whose plan resembles a phallos,[2] or the countless hot-dog stands shaped like hot-dogs. Is our shopping mall masquerading as a Roman apartment building simply a remarkably subtle and sophisticated transformation of the aforementioned (apparently) simple one-to-one mappings of "form and function?" The mind boggles at the task of having to reconstruct the latter out of the former.

Let us put these issues at rest for a moment and consider again the large building compound in which my cafe is situated. There are activities going on in all of its component space-cells which are unknown or unknowable to the users of any given cell. These activities are taking place "simultaneously," unknown to each other. 2:10 PM in space-cell M will have different contextual connotations from 2:10 PM in space-cell N.

We are situated in the midst of a bewilderingly complex space-time framework for human action and interaction. This framework, moreover, is no simple passive stage-set for activity. Its component parts actively engage our perceptions, challenging us at every turn, offering us possibilities for and constraints upon action and experience. A given component may have certain connotations for me when experienced from one direction rather than another. Spaces are perceived in subtly different ways at different times.

We are continually and relentlessly presented with experiential choices in the built environment, and yet we would appear to respond in ways which can only be partly "determined." In some bizarre fashion, we have built ourselves into a vast artifactual web, something which is both beehive and language at the same time, and yet somehow not quite either.

Let us look more closely at the environment I've been describing. The window of my cafe is set into a concrete pillar-bay or frame. The pillar to the left is painted blue, while that on the right is painted red. The window sill itself is painted white. In the clothing store to the right, all three components are painted white. In the shoe store beyond, the two pillars are painted red, and the sill off-white.

I am fully aware of these differences only some of the time, principally when navigating the street at a distance: the blue pillar which I see down the block serves to orient my groggy steps in the early morning when I come for my daily caffein dosage. I cross the street at an angle appropriate to depositing me at the cafe in a straight (diagonal) line.

So, it would appear that, for me at least, this coloring serves as a navigational guide—although only insofar as I myself have made such an association and duly employ it as such. I have not enquired of my fellow patrons what navigational aids they employ, which I assume to be anything from something equivalent to the above, to the aroma of warm croissants which can (sometimes) be sensed over the automobile exhaust fumes.

And yet I am certainly inconsistent in my usage of this color coding to tell me "where" I am: as I consider the question, I become aware that I employ an enormous number of visual, tactile and olfactory cues to guide my way about the town. I "know where I am" in the city by employing anything from certain consistent odors to minute changes in the patterns of pavement, not to speak of written signs. It would appear that almost anything palpable (street J is always windy in

Winter) may be so employed. To make up a taxonomy of such cues might be as useful—or as useless—as classifying all the oval objects in the universe.

My behavior is apparently inconsistent in this regard: I employ the "same" objects in different ways (but are they then the same?), and differently at different times. I employ a wide variety of cues even in the same street to help me navigate myself to the same place (is it then the "same" place?).

Moreover, what do I know of the "intentions" of those who may have structured these large or small components of the built environment? I am not so presumptuous as to assume that they were all put there for *my* benefit, and yet they *do* function on my behalf, even if they function differently for others. They are broadcast widely for all who would employ them in whatever ways they might conceivably be employed. This is not to say, however, that portions of this transmission are not privileged with regard to various receivers.

Let us consider the colored window frame of my coffeeshop. The red-white-blue pattern of the frame (for me at least) suggests associations with France, and I can dimly perceive a long line of associations—i.e., verbally linear, but somehow all visually simultaneous—with Parisian cafes, French cuisine, spirited conversation and/or silent people-watching, some indefinable "ambience."

It comes as a slight jolt to recall the name of the cafe: "Piroschka," recalling in fact Vienna and a legend about a little Hungarian girl. The proprietors are German-speaking, and inherited the place from a time when it was called (more appropriately?) "C'est si bon." Perhaps, then, the red, white and blue window frame is left over from the days of Gallic hegemony. But why is it retained and what purpose does the color-coding serve? Why not Austrian or Hungarian colors? The mind reels; maybe little Piroschka wore a red, white and blue dress (or was it blue, red and white?). Maybe the colors are intended to stand for the verbal message "Attention! French cuisine inside. Enter with haste (or caution)."

The more one presses the object for a coherent or at least relatively homogeneous message, the further away an answer seems: even the "French coffee" listed on the blackboard menu is "Medaglia D'Oro" Italian coffee. Bear in mind also, that the complex web of associations which I have begun to spin is my own (apparently) idiosyncratic web: the person at the next table will undoubtedly have her own web to spin. And both of ours may be widely divergent from the "intentions" of the owners, assuming theirs were homogeneous in any way in the first place. After all, they didn't build the place, they merely infilled an existing cubicle, and not all of that either, having inherited some furniture, appliances, and grocery purveyors: if memory serves, these are the same old croissants as in the old days.

It may be wise to put a halt to the peeling of this fruit before we reach what will undoubtedly be its hollow core, and attempt to regain some of our initial delight in the extraordinary complexity of the built environment. It may be useful to press the issue of our tricolor window frame in a somewhat more circumspect fashion.

We have noted that this color-coding exists in a wider context of window frames in the same building compound, each of which manifests certain *contrasts* with the others: ours is red, white and blue, that next door is all white, the one beyond is red, white and red, and so forth. We have a palpable, perceptible distinction in the coloring of the three window frames.

We will observe further that our tricolor window frame stands in a space-cell otherwise painted white (over brick). The neighboring space cells are composed of brick walls, one painted cream, the other white.

We would seem to have arrived at an obvious yet nonetheless remarkable observation: window frames (or space-cells, for that matter) *need not* be colored any one way. We can imagine (or observe) thousands of space-cell components around the city painted any which way, for no reason than anyone can figure out, except that in *some* cases a given color or color-combination may have certain conventional or symbolic associations: the crimson red so commonly found around the university is deliberately employed to make an association with the university and its name. But this association is completely arbitrary and conventional; moreover, there are objects painted crimson red in the city which are not thought of as associated with the university (even though some persons *may* conjure up an imaginary association if they so wish).

So, if objects need not be colored any one way, and may be colored variously, some of these colorings may be "symbolic" some of the time. And, equally, some will not be; some will be "meaningless" insofar as their presence serves merely to contrast their objects (or space-cells, or structures) from others. The established contrasts, moreover, may be connotative for any individual in a variety of ways (navigational or locational or directional aids, etc.), some or none of which may have been directly intended by those who painted or designed the objects.

We are left with an apparent paradox. It would seem that *at least some of the component objects in the built environment can be both "meaningful" and "meaningless" at the same time.* Or perhaps they can be "meaningful" in different ways (symbolic *or* merely contrastive). If we look more closely at the nature of this "contrastive" function, we would be hard put to assign any value to the context of the contrastive object (in this case coloring) apart from mere "otherness." The red in this object may be there solely to contrast with the adjacent green; if the adjacent object were red, the former might just as well be green. Or blue, yellow or white.

Hence, we might affirm that at least some portion of the built environment has at least some of its function that of creating perceptible or palpable *distinctions* or contrasts (for whatever reason distinctions may be required). The built world is addressed to human perceptual mechanisms which themselves function through the apprehension of contrast (edges, changes of color-region, and other discontinuities).

Indeed, it would appear to be fundamental to the nature of the built environment to create disjunctions, contrasts and discontinuities: every object, every space-cell, every locus of action and interaction, may be distinguished through its boundedness, separation or enclosure (by whatever physical or material means).

Consider that there are (or were, as the case may be) trolley barns in the city which do *not* masquerade as Roman blocks of flats. Consider also that non-trolley barns may also masquerade as the same. In some cases, even blocks of flats may masquerade as (Roman) blocks of flats.

Consider that two otherwise identical space-cells may be painted different colors. Consider also two identical space-cells painted the same colors, the first having rough-textured walls, the second smooth. Consider two space cells of identical geometric configuration (cubes), one 10 meters on a side, the other 12 meters on a side. Or consider again two space-cells of identical configuration, size, color, and texture. One is a barber shop, one a chapel.

Such examples highlight the fact that the built environment is a highly complex system organized in hierarchical fashion, with contrastive levels of organization, each level apparently in some sense semi-autonomous of the others, yet connected to one another in at least partly predictable ways, given certain conventions held in common at a given place and time.

In attempting to understand the organization of an architectonic formation, it will be important to be clear about the position or perspective of analysis. In the previous paragraphs we have suggested a number of perspectives on formations. It is evidently the case that the architectonic system, like any system of signs, manifests a property of conditional elementarity. That is to say, *in specifying what the component units of a formation are, that specification will be a function of the level of organization being addressed.*

ARCHITECTONIC ANALYSIS

The principal problem in establishing the nature of architectonic units is the specification of what is *invariant* across the often bewilderingly complex variations in form in a given built environment. As we experience the complex network of formal relationships which go to make up a particular settlement or its component parts, palpable similarities will arise—recognizable patterns of repeated forms or patterns of composition of various forms in a three-dimensional array. Certain "underlying regularities" become manifest on nearly any level of sensory experience. Often such regularities do not cross the boundaries of specific neighborhoods, while at times whole settlements manifest a homogeneity in formal appearance. The highly complex cognitive mapping or internal imagery which we as viewers and users often manifest in our memory of given places is partly idiosyncratic and partly held in common by others in a population.[1] What is it that constitutes the data of our perceptual structuration of environments? Or, to turn the question around, how do built environments *address* our perceptual and cognitive mechanisms, which have surely in some sense evolved to interact with these remarkable artifacts which our species has built itself into?

At the same time that we are interested in establishing groups of regularities or broad patterns of organization in specific architectonic systems, we are concerned with what may be held in common by architectonic systems in general. It will be clear that any set of "architectonic universals" will be a subset of the former. Architectonic analysis has as one of its aims the establishment of what might be justly termed the "design features" of human architecture, namely those features or properties of organization which simultaneously describe the architectonic system *per se* and distinguish it from "animal architecture" on the one hand[2] (assuming there are significant and palapable distinctions) as well as from other semiotic systems.

It would appear that every architectonic system shares at least this one thing in common: that they are made up of what we might call 'space-cells' (of a wide variety of geometric configurations and sizes). That is to say, portions of the spatial continuum are bound off from each other in a great variety of ways: spaces are enclosed, or mass-forms are so composed as to suggest enclosure of some sort. Human activities are localized in portions of the environment in relatively habitual ways.

An entire settlement may be seen as a complex space-time framework for human action and interaction. It is a spatio-temporal framework in that activities are framed or situated not only spatially but also sequentially. An architectural object of whatever size and complexity is "addressed" by routines of behavior which unfold over time and which often are sequentially situated in groups of space-cells composed in three-dimensional aggregates. The linear or multilinear geometry of behavioral episodes are, as it were, "mapped into" the multidimensional geometries of architectonic objects.

Furthermore, this interactive mapping of activity and built environment is simultaneously specific and arbitrary: at a given moment, a behavioral episode is mapped onto a specific space cell or across a group of space cells, and yet this association may be temporary, arbitrary and conventional in nature—at the next instance, what we might recognize as a similar or equivalent behavioral routine or activity is differently mapped. We manifest a remarkable ability to employ a given space cell for a variety of apparently contradictory activities. Given certain palpable physical constraints, we appear to be able to "use" almost any bounded space for almost any activity.

It would seem that spatial behavior and built environments manifest a certain semi-autonomous relationship—much less rigidly determined than that between the behaviors of certain social insects and their hives or nests—and yet somehow not entirely or completely arbitrary, being to some extent grounded in the routines of convention which differ from one society to another. Furthermore, even within the conventions of "behavioral mapping" apparently canonical to a given society, we may observe wide variations in usage among its members—certain spaces are minimally used by one sex, or used in palpably different ways, or used by various social moieties in different ways on festive occasions, contrasting with "secular" usages at other times, and so forth.

In addition, if we are to say that a built environment suggests certain "readings," then such "messages" may be decoded inside-out or upside-down, unilinearly or as a series of simultaneous embeddings, and so forth. In certain instances, a built form may suggest a "grammatical" procedure for its spatially-sequenced "unfolding," but this may not necessarily mean that we cannot experience its organization "backwards." The space-cells of a compound are rarely composed of moving walkways going in only one (or two) directions, and a given cell may participate in the intersection of a large number of experiential routines.

Hence, while existing as objects composed of parts simultaneously "given," architectural artifacts may be experienced, read or decoded in ways which may be multidimensional and multisequential in the extreme, in conventional and idiosyncratic ways. But it is evident that not every corpus allows the same degree of interpretative freedom.[3]

Let us return to the question of the nature of architectonic units. We have asserted that what may be held in common by all architectonic systems is an entity we may term the *space-cell* or *space-frame* manifesting a topological property of *boundedness*. Hence in a very general manner, all space-cells are *equivalent* in a topological sense. It is simultaneously apparent that space-cells differ along what might be termed a *geometric* axis. In other words, from a topological perspective, two space cells will be equivalent though they may differ markedly in their formal or geometric realization, i.e., from a geometric perspective; X is a cube while Y is a cylinder.

It will be immediately apparent that two cubic cells, X and X', will be equivalent geometrically while exhibiting variation in material or physical expression: X is constructed in ferroconcrete while X' is realized in wood, or brick, or animal skins, or may be simply marked out by twelve logs arranged horizontally and vertically, without infilled "walls."

We can carry out this variation even further: cubic cell X, realized in brick, may contrast with cubic cell X', realized in brick which has been painted blue. Or, X may be a cubic cell 3 meters on a side, while X' may be a cubic cell 4 meters on a side (whether or not both are brick, or even if they are brick and painted brick).

It will be clear that equivalent geometric forms may exhibit variation on a wide variety of realizational axes, and two geometrically equivalent cells may contrast as to media, texture, color, absolute size, and so forth. It would also seem clear, at least intuitively, that such variation is in some sense "meaningful"; i.e., that within the conventions suggested by a given social group, variations in form or material expression are intended to be matched by variations in meaning or function or association, however subtly.

The nature of this "matching" is of course highly complex, and resists being forced into a simplistic "form follows function" mold *or* into a completely arbitrary and idiosyncratic model. As we shall see in the course of the present study, the literature on "architectural meaning" is a mare's nest of conflicting proposals and *ad hoc* suggestions on the part of social scientists, anthropologists, art historians, and architectural semioticians. (At the same time, there is so much that is intuitively insightful in the traditional literature that we would ignore it at great peril.)

The principal problem facing the analyst of built environments is "what is it that is constant (invariant) across a given array?" and, correlatively, "what are the parameters of variation which formative disjunctions undergo?"

In order to measure variation, the analyst will necessarily apply to an array some constant measure or *frame* within which variation can be highlighted and classified. Clearly, the choice of a reference frame will crucially determine the course of an analysis and the nature of its salient results. To be sure, at the outset of an analysis, the choice of reference frame may be more or less intuitively made, as it is evident that the process of measuring variation will simultaneously serve to clarify the conception and formation of the reference frame itself.

It should be maximally productive if the frame of reference is in some useful sense a simple abstraction of some recurrent formative component in arrays, a component which moreover appears to recur generally from one code to another.

As we have observed above, what is common to any built environment is some geometric transform of what we will call the *space-cell*, namely a co-occurrent mass-and-space formation revealing an overall property of boundedness. Such an entity comprises a contrastive opposition of simultaneously- occurrent and mutually-defining masses and volumes, defining a topological unity.

From the point of view of such a primitive entity, all the space-cells of an architectonic system will be topologically equivalent. In other words, behind the variations in geometric formation (and of course in material articulation or realization), all space-cells in a corpus will share a topological property of boundedness.

In order for the notion of the space-cell to be sufficiently general, it is necessary to distinguish it carefully from the geometric or formal concept expressed by (for example) the English lexical item "room," which generically refers to a spatial or volumetric configuration delimited or bounded by one or more masses. The notion of the space-cell will also include the *obverse* of a "room," or mass-bounded volume, namely space-bounded masses, or an object and its 'surround.' Moreover, a cell may result more generically from place-making constructions generated solely by bodies themselves.

Thus, formations as geometrically various as the following will be considered as equivalent in a cellular perspective:

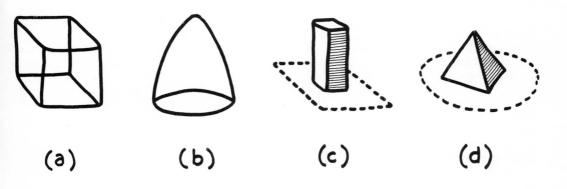

(a)   (b)   (c)   (d)

Clearly, this is not to exclude other perspectives which will distinguish (a) and (b); or (a,b) and (c,d); or (a,c) and (b,d).

Furthermore, we may distinguish a series of space-cells $(a_1, a_2, a_3 \ldots a_n)$ wherein *geometrically*-equivalent cells contrast in terms of (1) absolute size, (2) constructional material, (3) color, (4) texture, and so forth. Each of the latter may provisionally be regarded as providing contrastive perspectives (or axes of contrast). Thus, (a_1) and (a_2) may share the same geometric formation as well as the same size (1), but may be widely divergent in terms of medium, color and texture (2,3,4);—i.e., materially.

In addition, two space-cells which are geometrically and materially identical may be associated with quite different functions or usages, and, furthermore, this contrast may or may not be correlated with contextual differences of relative placement in multicellular compound.

It will be evident that the analyst is dealing with objects which in various ways display a variety of component features or properties of formation, and that the task of analysis is concerned in part with establishing the diverse ways in which some properties of a given formation will contrast with some properties of another formation. In this way, we will come to understand the ways in which two isolated portions of an array may be *both* similar and different.

In addition, architectonic objects reveal component features of formation which are significant in different ways. A complex object such as a building may be constituted such that certain of its component elements are *directly* significative, while others may be significative only in concert with other elements.

For example, the use of certain colors or materials may be directly associated with the identity of a given social class or with membership in a certain kinship group. In such a case, the presence of that material will be contrastively opposed to other materials which will be differently significative. Thus, the color crimson may be associated with an aristocratic clan, standing in opposition to (a) all other colors, which may or may not be specifically associated with other social groups, or (b) it may be successively opposed to other colors (as where crimson : blue :: aristocracy : merchant class, and crimson : green :: aristocracy : military, and so forth).

Furthermore, there may be cases where crimson-in-context X (limestone masonry) contrasts with crimson-in-context Y (timber frame construction; or where crimson + limestone masonry + curvilinear space-cells contrasts with crimson + timber frame construction + curvilinear *and/or* rectilinear space-cells.

In addition, other kinds of contextual conditions will modify the significative presence of a given material or geometric formation (such as location in an urban fabric, relationships with other buildings—contiguous *vs.* isolated, or directly on a street *vs.* removed from a street, etc.). The analyst will discover a highly complex hierarchy of significative associations wherein large numbers of elements in an array are ordered with respect to each other in many different ways, providing members of a society with an enormously varied set of associations and grades of significative modification.

In a similar fashion, but with quite different means, a verbal utterance will provide a listener with a great deal of information, e.g., about the referential context of a message or other orientations toward various components of the message in a functional sense,[4] and many different formative components of the message may signal information about the social class, emotional state, etc., of a speaker and/or the speaker's covert opinions regarding a given referent. Such aspects of the utterance as intonation, syntactic usage, phonological clarity, and so forth, may be directly significative in a wide variety of code-specific ways.

Architectonic objects are normally composed of various sign-types such that the overall significance of the object comprises a complex set of divergent associations. This may be easily demonstrated by a consideration of what constitutes "house" or domestic structure in one's own culture. This may include (a) characteristic cellular formations (or the exclusion of certain types of formations); (b) characteristic sequences of cells, either (1) geometrically or (2) functionally; (c) the use of certain kinds of materials, colors, finishings, sizes, etc., or the exclusion of various kinds; (d) characteristic types of infrastructural fittings (furniture, with its own patterns of allowable interrelationships, mechanical support systems, etc.); (e) characteristic relationships to an urban fabric (e.g., if contiguous with other houses, minimal separation from a public street, or if isolated from other houses, set back behind walls, gardens, etc.); (f) characteristic sizes and positions of formative components such as windows, doors, stairwells, etc.; (g) the presence or exclusion of various kinds of symbolic motifs redundantly signifying domesticity.[5]

The following example may serve to illustrate the kinds of formative complexity typical in an architectonic code.

FORMATIVE UNITS

Plates I through VIII consist of isometric reconstructions of the groundplans of several contemporaneous domestic buildings erected on the island of Crete ca. 1500 B.C. Of interest here are the series of space-cells labelled in each diagram (a)(b)(c), known in the archaeological literature as "Minoan hall systems," associated generally with the private domestic quarters of Minoan houses.[6]

The structures have been taken from several towns on the island, and are chosen at random to illustrate some of the variety of formations evident in the corpus. The buildings are referred to in the following analysis by their conventional names as fancifully assigned by their excavators. They are:

I.   Akhladhia, House A (abbreviated below as AKHL)
II.   Knossos, House of the Chancel Screen (KN HCS)
III.   Knossos, the Royal Villa (KN RV)
IV.   Knossos, the House of the Frescoes (KN HF)
V.   Mallia, House Delta Alpha (ML DA)
VI.   Mallia, House Zeta Alpha (ML ZA)
VII.   Tylissos, House A (TYL A)
VIII.   Tylissos, House C (TYL C)

In the first example (AKHL) we are concerned with cells (a,b,c) and their relationship to adjacent aggregates (m-n) and (g-h).

The hall system consists of (c-b-a) : entrance to the system is from vestibule (h) via a double door opening both into the left-hand cell and the central cell (a,b). Cell (a) is formally realized with its right-hand side as a colonnade (/c/); cell (b) with its left-hand side that colonnade and right-hand side a pier-and-door partition (henceforth referred to as /PDP/); the right-hand cell (c) with its left-hand side a /PDP/.

Cell (c) may have been a dining room: it contains an L-shaped bench on the two far walls, and (c) abuts two smaller cells (m,n) which appear to have been a kitchen and pantry. All three cells of the system (a,b,c) connect with cells to the side flank of the system (h,h/g,g, respectively). The portion of cell (g) connected to system cell (b) is paved with flagstones (the rest of the floors in the house are beaten earth), and may have been a small lightwell. If cell (a) was similar to equivalent cells at TYL, it too may have been a lightwell.

The second house (KN HCS, *Plate* II) reveals a similar pattern (cells (a-b-c)), but here cell (c) is connected laterally to a curious cell (d) with a raised dias on a platform, of unknown usage. Entrance to the system is, similar to AKHL, laterally into the central cell (b). Here, however, the wall-position between cells (a) and (b) is not realized as a colonnade but as a /PDP/. There *is* a colonnade separating cells (c) and (d) however.

The third house (KN RV, *Plate* III.) has the arrangement familiar at AKHL A (cells (a-b-c)), plus a fourth cell (d) beyond (c) and behind a balustrade, of unknown usage.

The fourth (KN HF, *Plate* IV.) has a hall system of three components (a-b-c), where again cell (a) is a lightwell (as in the previous example), but its separation from (b) is not a colonnade but a /PDP/ plus a wall-extension, and the separation of (b) and (c), originally perhaps a /PDP/, is now a wall with two doors.

The fifth example (ML DA, *Plate* V.) has the familiar arrangement (cells (a-b-c)), and entrance is gained through the right-hand cell (c) via a /PDP/.

The sixth (ML ZA, *Plate* VI.) is identical to the previous except that cell (a), a lightwell in ML DA, is here a garden; but entrance is similarly gained through right-hand cell (c) (a single door, however, and not a /PDP/.

The seventh and eighth (TYL A & C, *Plates* VII. and VIII.) are also similar, the hall systems in TYL A being cells (a-b-c) and in TYL C being cells (a-b-c).

We will refer to the three components of all the hall systems as the "a" cell (or lightwell), the "b" cell (or middle room or "porch"), and the "c" cell (or "hall"), and the notations in our *Plates* are identical on this count.

Clearly, we are dealing with a constant or invariant cellular 'syntax' (a-b-c) across a number of contextual variants or alternative formal realizations. Note the following correspondences:

	a		b		c
AKHL A	lightwell (?)	/C/	porch	/PDP/	hall
KN HCS	lightwell	/PDP/	porch	/PDP/	hall
KN RV	lightwell	/C/	porch	/PDP/	hall
KN HF	lightwell	/PDP/	porch	doors*	hall
ML DA	lightwell	/C/	porch	/PDP/	hall
ML ZA	garden	/C/	porch	/PDP/	hall
TYL A	lightwell	/C/**	porch	/PDP/	hall
TYL C	lightwell	/C/	porch	/PDP	hall

*Apparently originally a /PDP/.
**L-shaped colonnade, or "/C/".

Table 1. Formal Cellular Realization

The internal syntactic aggregation of all examples is the same, but there are alternative formal realizations, as the *Table* above indicates :

(1) the (a-b) boundary may be *either* /C/ or /PDP/;
(2) the (a) cell is invariantly an "outdoor" or unroofed cell (or a cell with a clerestorey roof), but may be *either* an enclosed open area ("garden," as in ML ZA) or a relatively small lightwell. Hence there may be alternative *formal* realizations. In the hall systems of the two large "palaces" of Mallia and Phaistos,[7] we find both a lightwell and a "garden."
(3) The (a-b) boundary realized formally as /C/ may be *either* L-shaped (TYL A) or unilinear (all others).
(4) In the example of KN HF, the (a-b) boundary is not only a /PDP/ and not a /C/, but it is only *partly* a /PDP/.

In our examination of TYL A and C we arrive at the tentative conclusion that there was an apparent invariance within the hall systems with respect to relative *size* of cells: at TYL, the (b) cell was the smallest, the (c) cell the largest.

But if we take all of the examples into consideration, it will be evident that this size-ratio is not invariant. In the next *Table*, "1" = largest cell, "2" = middle-sized, and "3" = smallest cell:

	a	b	c
AKHL A		all equal in size	
KN HCS	3	2	1
KN RV	2	2	1
KN HF	2	1	3
ML DA	2	2	1
ML ZA	1	3	2
TYL A	2	3	1
TYL C	2	3	1

Table 2. Relative Size

Evidently, then, the relative size of the (a-b-c) cells is not invariant. Consequently, there will be *alternative material realizations* with respect to size (modularity), or what may be termed contextual variance.

Let us look at several other aspects or features which may be invariant across our examples.

With respect to the manner of access to the hall system—i.e., its syntactic position with respect to other aggregates—it will be seen that primary access (i.e., from cells leading to the building's entrance) is as follows:

	a		b		c
AKHL A	x	and	x		
KN HCS			x		
KN RV	x			or	x
KN HF	x	or	x		
ML DA					x
ML ZA					x
TYL A			x		
TYL C					x

Table 3. Primary Access

Evidently, access from the outside may be gained into any of the three cells, and in two cases into more than one: at AKHL A, entrance-vestibule (h) has a door opening into (a) and one opening into (b); at KN HF, house vestibule (f) has two doors: one leads into a corridor (e-d) leading to (a), another into a series of cells (h-i) which lead into cell (b).

But what is *invariant,* however, is the fact that in *all* examples, *access is lateral to the longitudinal axis of the system.*

It will be noted that in all cases, the hall systems do not open directly onto a street or primary house entrance, but are at least one cell removed from that entrance: in the following *Table*, the access to the system is shown with respect to how many thresholds (doorways) separate it from the primary house entrance (E).

	Number of thresholds including house door	
AKHL A	2	(= 1 cell separation)
KN HCS	2	(1)
KN RV	2	(1)
KN HF	4	(3)
ML DA	3	(2)
ML ZA	4	(3)
TYL A	4	(3)
TYL C	4	(3)

Table 4. Separation from Outside

In other words, there is *invariantly* a minimum of *one cell* between hall system and house door (or two doors), and the system may be as many as *three* cells removed, possibly more depending on the size of the house. But no matter how small the house, there is always *at least* one intermediary cell.

Thus far, we might specify the formative features of the hall system as consisting of

(1)   an aggregate of 3 cells of type (a-b-c)
(2)   in a linear sequence (a) + (b) + (c)
(3)   lateral to direction of access
(4)   forming a portion of a larger aggregate such that the system is 1 or 1+ cells removed from entry into the overall aggregate

It will be understood in (1) that the cells are contiguous, and share party walls (a/b and b/c). We have seen above (*Table* 1.) and (p. 18) the range of formal realizations of the cells regarding such party walls (/C/, /PDP/).

There are other features closely connected with the hall systems, notably the presence of stairwells to a second storey. These occur either in a cell adjacent to one of the cells in the system (but never (a)), or open directly into one of the cells:

	stair	off cell	in cell no.
AKHL A	*	c	g
KN HCS	x	b	i
KN RV	x	c	g
KN HF	**	b	i
ML DA	x	c	g
ML ZA	x	c	d
TYL A	x	c	onto c
TYL C	x	c	m

*At AKHL, it is conjectured that there was a stair in cell (g).
**At KN HF, there may have been a stair in cell (i).

Table 5. Associated Stairwells

In all cases, the stairwell is closely associated with the (c) or (b) cells of the system, and is, more-over, distinct from stair wells(s) which serve more "public" portions of a house. In other words, the hall system-stairwell is one of controlled access, behind doorways which are "beyond" (with respect to outside entrance into the house) the system itself. In several cases (TYL A & C, KN RV) there are two private stairs nearby.

The houses also have several other types of cell, often closely associated with the hall systems, though not invariably so:

(1)   "pillar crypts" or shrines:
      KN HCS (h), off (i) off (b)
      KN RV (e), off (c)

(2)   pillar rooms, perhaps not shrines:
      AKHL A (i), off (h) off (b or a) (workshop?)
      TYL A (p), off (b)
      TYL C (p)   (workshop?)

(3)   washing/lustral cells and/or latrines:
           AKHL A (f) = latrine?
           KN HCS (f) = (sunken) bath
           KN RV (h) = latrine?
           ML DA (f) = (sunken) bath
           ML ZA (g) = (sunken) bath; (h) = latrine
           TYL A (d) = latrine?
           TYL C (f) = latrine

In addition to the connections providing access into the hall systems, principally from the primary house entrance, some cells in various systems provide connections elsewhere in the house:

off:	(a)	(b)	(c) ,	into how many cells
AKHL A	(P)	(P) + 1	3	
KN HCS	1	(P) + 1	1	
KN RV	(P)		3	
KN HF	(P)	(P)		
ML DA		(P)	1	
ML ZA	**		(P)	
TYL A		(P) + 2	4 + stair	
TYL C	*		(P) + 1	

*In (a) in TYL C is a window opening into an adjacent cell.
**It is not known if the garden here opens onto other cells in adjacent buildings.
(P) = "primary access."

Table 6. Secondary Access

Consequently, several cells in the systems have at least a *dual* function: as a component in the system itself, and as a *passageway* to other cells outside the system (apart from connections to primary access ((P) above). In TYL A, for example, cell (b) serves simultaneously as a "b" cell and as a segment in a continuing corridor "bisecting" the system. In KN RV, cell (c) provides access to 3 cells, and serves as a segment in the passage from the left to the right side of the structure.

We have to add to our list of formative features of the hall system given above the following:

(5)   the system is not self-contained with respect to other cellular aggregates, but may function as a passageway to other aggregates.

The following diagram (*Figure* 1.) portrays the invariant sequential order of the formative features of the hall system:

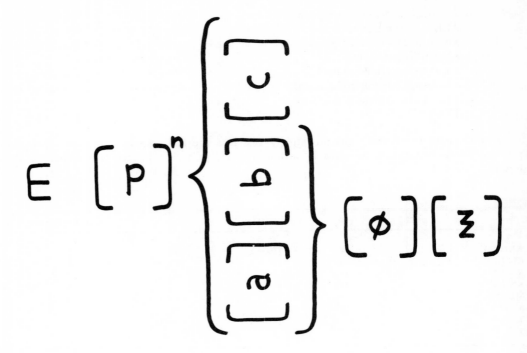

$$E \; [P]^n \left\{ \begin{bmatrix} c \end{bmatrix} \begin{bmatrix} b \end{bmatrix} \begin{bmatrix} a \end{bmatrix} \right\} [\phi] [\mathsf{Z}]$$

E : EXTERIOR   P : PRIMARY ACCESS ϕ : ONE CELL Z : STAIRWELL

Figure 1

(understanding the range of formal and material alternative realizations of (a-b-c)).

Hence the formative features of the Minoan hall system include

(A)   the specified set of components (a), (b), (c), and their formal (and material) contextual variants;

(B)   an ordering or structure of those components, as specified in *Figure* 1.

Included in both (A) and (B) are series of formal, material and syntactic constraints as specified in the discussions in this section. Thus, the specification of lateral access to the system in (B) implies the formal realization of at least one doorway in at least one wall of one (or two) cells, and so forth. The specification of (a) as lightwell implies the material realization of formal item —as here, *viz., floor*—as a cement or stone pavement, etc.

Let us now consider a comparative example and examine the manner in which other houses in another corpus are organized in terms of formative features.

Plates IX. and X. are plans of two Egyptian houses, at el-Lahun and Amarna. The former, dated to the reign of the Pharoah Sesostris II, in the Nineteenth Century B.C. is a row house in a planned village built in association with construction of that Pharoah's pyramid. That at Amarna is a detached house in a yard, the residence of a bureaucrat known as the vizier Nakht.

The latter is considerably smaller than the former, and has many fewer rooms; it was constructed in the Fourteenth Century B.C., or some five or six centuries after the former.

Despite wide differences in size and layout, the two houses reveal a number of similarities—pillared halls of several types, for example, arranged in sequence. But the interrelations of the various cells appear very different in the two houses:

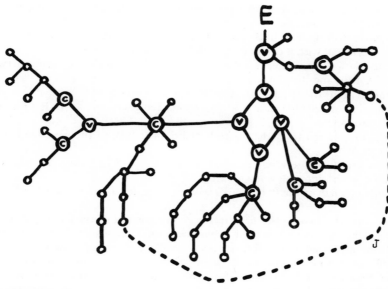

E : EXTERIOR

Ⓥ : VESTIBULE

Ⓒ : COURT / LIGHT WELL

EL·LAHUN

AMARNA

Figure 2

The networks of cells (their syntactic aggregation) is quite distinct; except for one connection ("j" in our diagram) which makes a looped "string,"[a] el-Lahun is organized strictly as a series of terminal "strings." On the other hand, Amarna reveals a mixed organization of terminal and looped "strings" (i.e., concatenated sequences of space-cells), including a loop within a loop, reminiscent of characteristic Minoan organizations.

What is constant across these aggregations are the following features (refer to the plans in *Plates* IX. and X.):

(1)   Amarna (AMR):2 small square cells immediately abutting the primary entrances (a,b); el-Lahun (ELL) has two similar cells, but they are separated by a long north-south corridor with two halves (x);

(2)   The second vestibule in both cases opens onto a large cell: a colonnaded court at ELL, a hypostyle hall with 8 columns at AMR (cells (c) in both plans);

(3)   To the south of the latter is a 4-columned hall (d) in both houses; but between (c) and (d) at AMR is another cell (cd);

(4)   To the south of the latter is a one-columned hall (f) in both houses;

(5)   To the side of cells (d) is, at ELL, a colonnaded court, and at AMR a 6-columned hall: (e) in both plans;

(6)   To the east of cell (f) is the master's bedroom (mbd), to the west the mistresses' bedroom (fbd);

(7)   A connection with servant's quarters is made at (j) in ELL, into the master's area, and, at AMR, at (k), into the women's area;

(8)   To the inner hall of the (mbd/fbd) areas are appended a series of small cells.

It is evident that the two houses have in common a great deal—the identity of given cells and their relative sequencing, as well as their deployment on a north-south axis, corresponding to a progression from larger and more public spaces to smaller and more private spaces, diverging into two private sub-zones, a men's quarters (on the east) and a women's quarters (on the west).

It becomes apparent that the long north-south corridor at ELL is needed to bring the progress of entrance onto a "fixed" north-south progression. Because ELL stands on the north side of a street, the visitor must be brought around to the north side of the house before being allowed to penetrate into the private dwelling areas. Similar houses on the south side of the street at ELL don't have the same problem, and the long corridor is absent.

The houses differ markedly in that where (c) or (e) are columned *halls* at AMR, they are *courtyards* at ELL. Perhaps because AMR stands in a large walled yard, outdoor courts within the structural frame of the building are unnecessary; ELL is a town house packed tightly alongside others.

But the relative positions of (c) and (e) in both houses are identical, and in the case of (c) its long axis is perpendicular to the long axis of the progression (c)-(d)-(f); in the case of (e), in both cases it approximates the size and proportions of (d) to its side, even though (e) in ELL is a court, and (e) in AMR is a hypostyle hall.

In addition, the relative proportions of (c), (d), (e), (f) are constant, and the sizes of (mbd) and (fbd) are similar in both houses.

We might portray the sequential or syntagmatic ordering of the formative features of the two houses as follows:

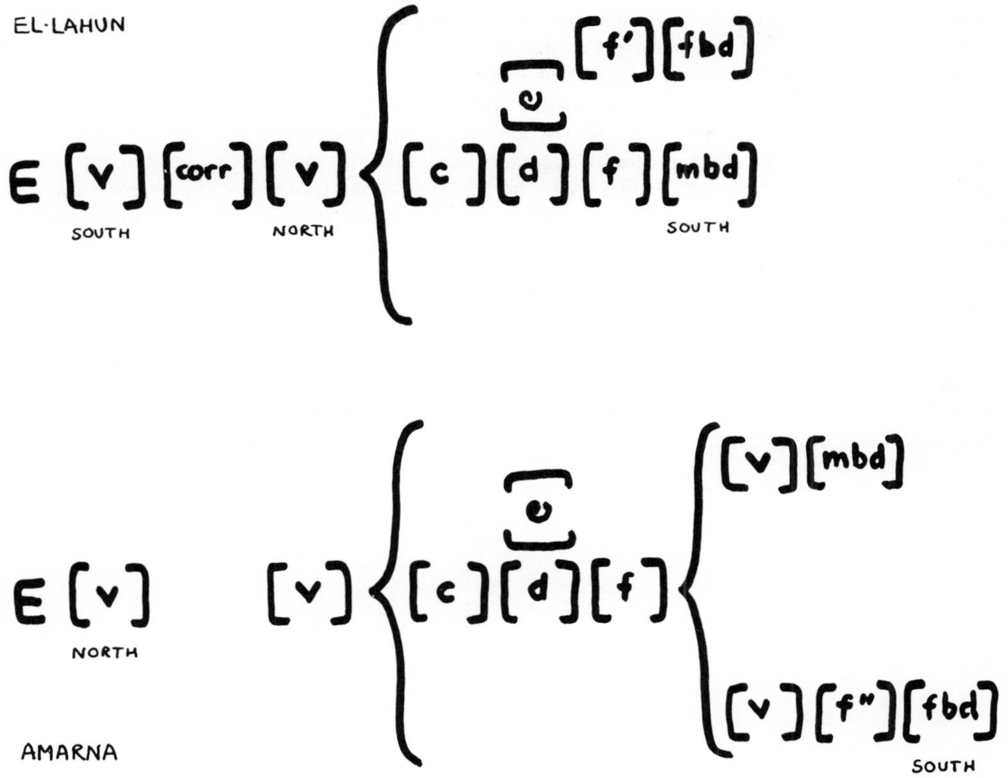

EL·LAHUN

$$E \; [v] \; [corr] \; [v] \; \left\{ \; [c] \; [d] \; [f] \; [mbd] \; \underset{\displaystyle \overset{\frown}{\smile}\,v}{}\; [f'] \; [fbd] \right.$$

SOUTH   NORTH   SOUTH

$$E \; [v] \quad [v] \left\{ \; [c] \; [d] \; [f] \left\{ \begin{array}{l} [v] \; [mbd] \\ \\ [v] \; [f''] \; [fbd] \end{array} \right. \right.$$

NORTH

AMARNA   SOUTH

Figure 3

Compare *Figures* 1. and 3. It will be evident how the formative *features* comprising the Minoan hall system differ from those comprising the Egyptian hall system, as well as how the *orderings* of those features contrast in both cases. Note with respect to the latter that whereas the Minoan system is invariant with respect to *lateral* access, the Egyptian system is invariant with respect to cardinal *orientation* (north-south progression from outer, public spaces to inner private spaces); the Minoan system lies perpendicular to the main direction of access from the exterior (E), while the Egyptian system lies along the same longitudinal, linear access. The Minoan system manifests variability with respect to connection of access to hall components, while the Egyptian system is invariably accessed at the largest, outermost cell. The Egyptian system, furthermore, bifurcates into two roughly identical aggregates, one associated with a male domain, the other with a female domain; no such bifurcation is apparent in the Minoan system (but note that we don't know what went on on the second storey (absent in these Egyptian houses), in the organization of private sleeping quarters (or summer sleeping quarters?).

Two examples hardly constitute a corpus, and our intent has been principally to suggest the directions of an ongoing and more comprehensive analysis. Nor is it implied here that the formative (or significative) structure constant across these two examples will not be modified by further analysis, no matter how remarkable it may seem that these two houses, separated in time by nearly 500 years, are apparently so similar in organization. Our aim here has been merely to provide a contrastive example to what was discovered above in the examination of the Minoan houses, and, through this, to suggest some of the dimensions whereby architectonic codes will contrast with each other on many levels of formative organization.

Architectonic codes employ as significant distinctions in form only *part* of the total number of *possible* distinctions which could be made. Furthermore, what is significant in one code may be non-significative in another code. As the above examples demonstrate, the cardinal orientation of a matrix of cells in an idiomatic aggregate is significant in the Egyptian corpus but non-significant in the Minoan. In the former case, there is a correlation between the orientation of the cellular matrix *north- : -south :: more public- : -more private.* In the latter case, *more private* is signified by an assemblage of certain diverse features of formation and their alternative realizations. Thus, the hall system is either physically far-removed from a house entrance, *or,* if relatively close, is approachable through multiple doors *and/or* by abrupt 90-degree changes of direction, etc.

The comparative analysis of architectonic corpora will highlight the evident conventionality of signification and the code-specificity of meaningful formation. In the next section we will explore further the notion of code-specific significance, and propose a system for the classification of architectonic signs.

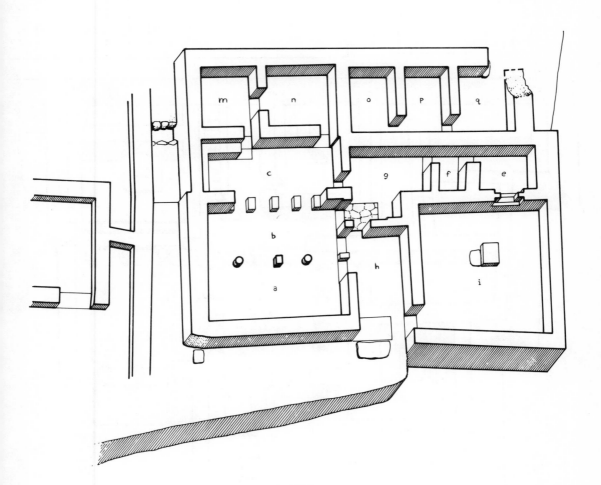

PLATE I

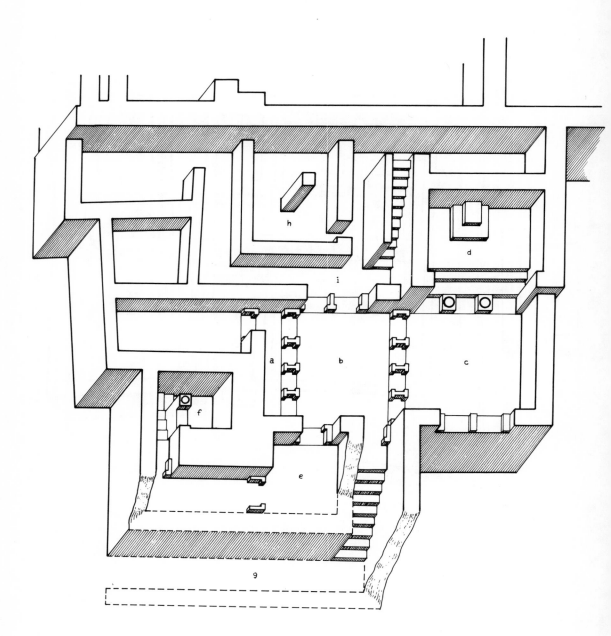

PLATE II

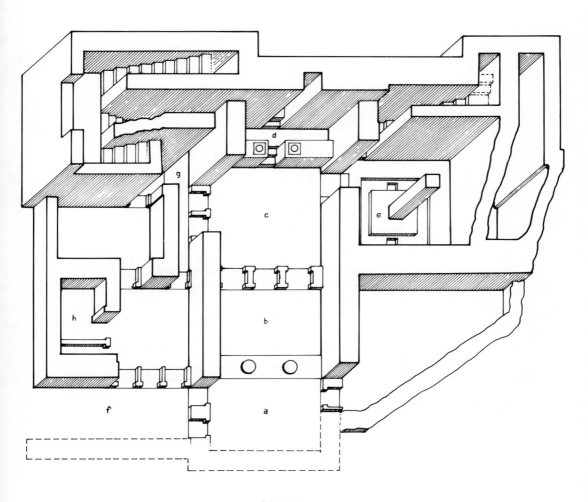

PLATE III

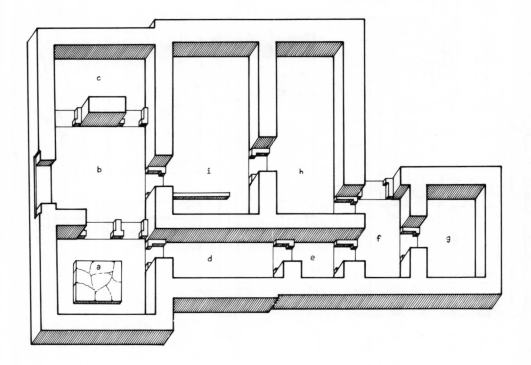

PLATE IV

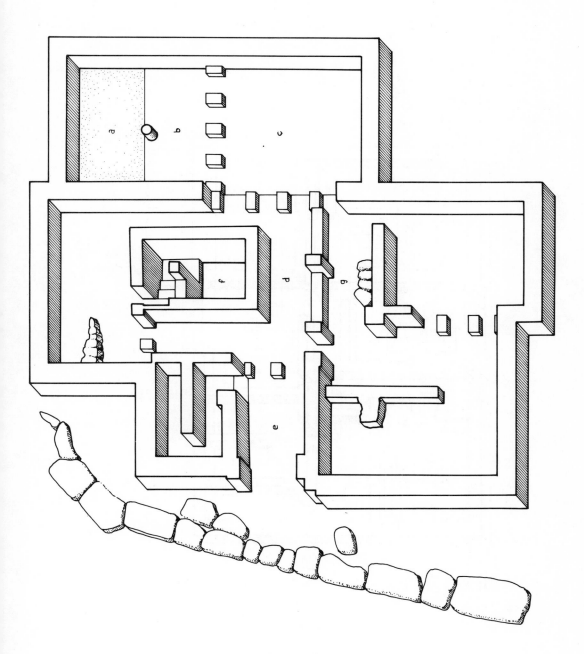

PLATE V

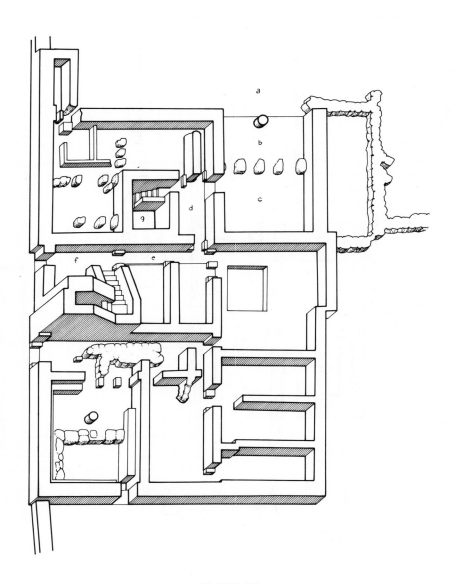

PLATE VI

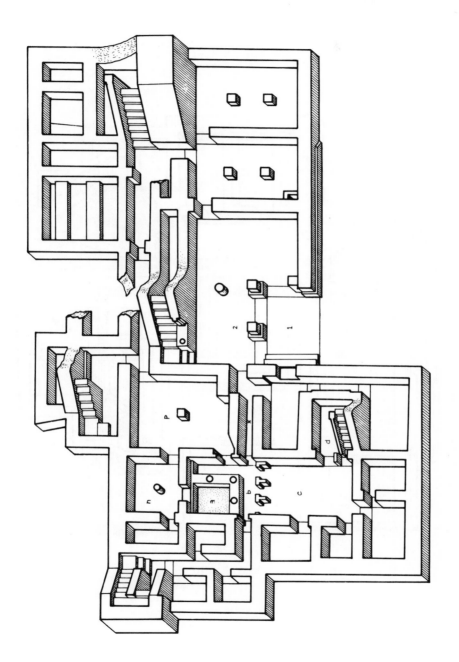

PLATE VII

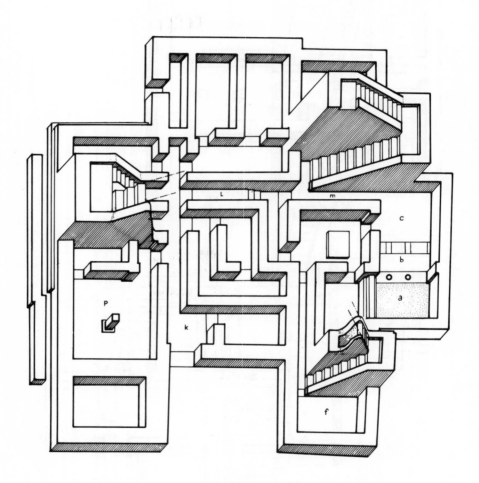

PLATE VIII

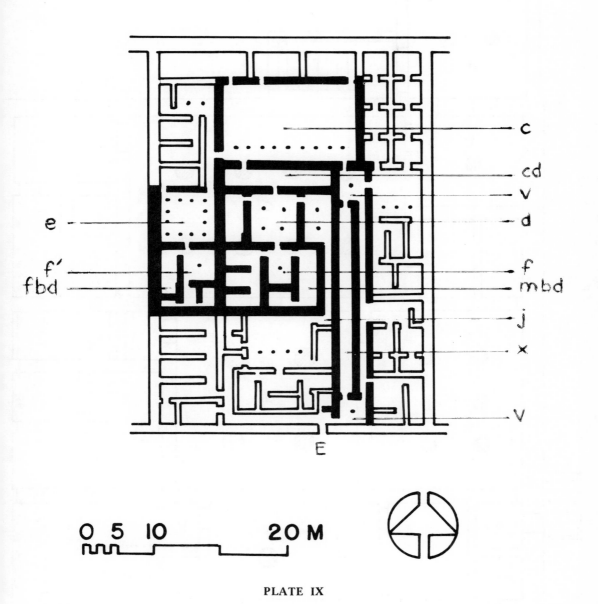

PLATE IX

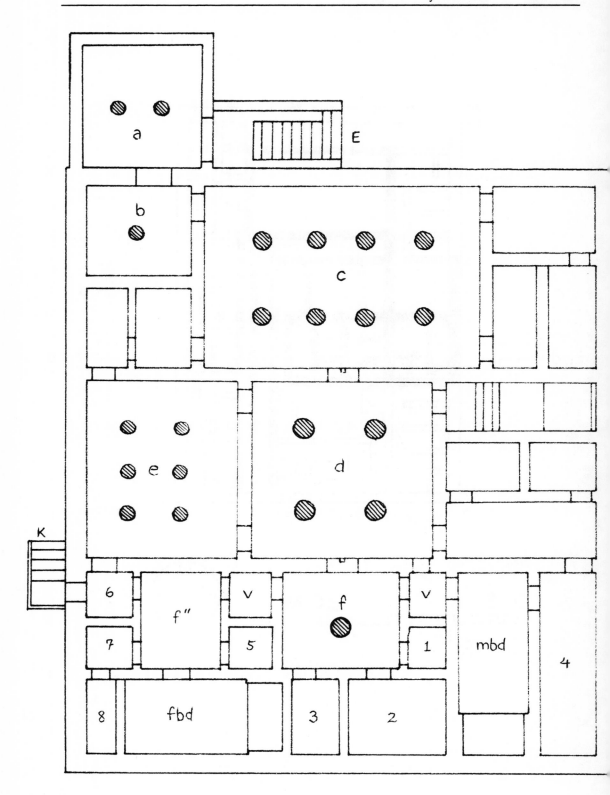

PLATE X

FOOTNOTES

CHAPTER II

[1] A great deal of important research has been carried out in recent years on the subject of cognitive mapping. A keystone in this work is K. Lynch's *The Image of the City*, Cambridge, Mass., 1960; see also the same writer's *What Time is This Place?*, Cambridge, Mass., 1975. In our bibliography below we have listed a number of especially important studies in this area, one of the most important frontiers of architectonic research. Particularly insightful is the theoretical and experimental work reported by Moore, Downs, Stea, Rapoport and others in recent years.

[2] On the subject of comparative architectonics, see the discussions in Preziosi, 1978c.

[3] We are accustomed in the highly eclectic built environments of the Western world to a rather wide range of free variation in interpretative association, but this is not the case in traditional societies, or in the Western world in the past. This is an important question, but we must take care not to confuse the trees for the forest, for it may well be that our apparent freedom for 'idiosyncratic' interpretation is itself carefully circumscribed. This remains a salient issue for future study.

[4] See, on architectonic function, our Chapter on Meaning below, and Preziosi, 1978c, Chapter III, and *id.*, 'The Parameters of the Architectonic Code,' 1978f, forthcoming, in the journal *Ars Semeiotica*, 1978.

[5] An interesting, albeit simplistically behavioristic, introduction to the subject of house-symbolism, may be found in C. C. Marcus, 'The House as Symbol of Self,' in *Designing for Human Behavior*, 1974, 130-146.

[6] This material has been chosen as an *exemplary* corpus of data in part because of field work done by the writer in this area, involving a detailed survey of some two hundred structures over several seasons. This work is reported in detail in the writer's doctoral dissertation, *Minoan Palace Planning and its Origins*, Harvard University, 1968 (see Bibliography below). The Minoan system has also been chosen as an exemplar because of its relatively limited extent (in contrast to the highly complex environments of modern urban settlements), involving the handling of only a few thousand cellular items, plus the fact that in contrast to systems elsewhere at that time, it reveals a great deal of formative complexity. No two Minoan buildings are identical, and the amount of formal and material variation in the corpus is very great. Another reason for the choice is historically sentimental: Minoan settlements comprise the first large-scale complex townscapes in Europe. Since the time of these analyses, work has been carried out in a variety of other corpora, both contemporary and historical. Reports on these are currently in preparation.

[7] The large central megastructures in Minoan cities, commonly called 'palaces' in the archaeological literature, also incorporated residential apartments sharing formative features with the Minoan houses looked at here (however else these megastructures functioned).

Chapter III
The Hierarchy of Signs

CELLS, MATRICES AND FORMS

The foregoing analyses, which comprise a portion of an ongoing analysis of architectonic codes by the writer and others, have served to illustrate the evident fact that the question of signification in the built environment is a function of the level of organization of a code. We have thus far noted the existence of at least two major levels of signification, or two types of architectonic signs: the *space-cell* and *matrices* of cellular aggregation.

The space-cell comprises a fundamental meaningful unity in a code, a sign type which moreover achieves distinctive modifications depending upon its association with sequences of cells. In the case of the Minoan corpus, the individual cell types (labelled above (a,b,c)) occur both singly and in the a-b-c sequence comprising the so-called Hall System. In these two cases, each cell functions in a different manner—i.e., cell type (a) is differently significative according to its occurrence as a single item (or in other cellular aggregates) or as a component in the a-b-c system.

The *space-cell*[a] enters into a variety of higher-level formations which are significative in various ways. Cells (in a corpus such as the two just looked at) aggregate into patterned sequences of cells or cell-*matrices* (such as a domestic hall-system). Larger units or *structures* may comprise separate buildings—i.e., sets of cells or matrices governed by controlled points of juncture or intersection, standing in opposition to other equivalent formations. Separate structures may (to continue our discussion in the context of the Minoan corpus) be either isolated or contiguous to other structures (sharing common mass-boundaries or party walls).

Above the level of the individual structure, characteristic formations may comprise *neighborhoods* of structures organized into patterned *grids* or blocks of varying types of configuration. Each corpus may exhibit one or more grid types with contrastive geometric configurations, often within the boundaries of a single urban fabric or settlement. Each corpus, and each settlement within a corpus, may reveal characteristic properties of formation including particular patterns of segregation of formative or functional types; neighborhoods may be walled off from each other (as in traditional Chinese or Peruvian cities; Hardoy, 1973, 380 ff.),[1] or may be distinguished on the basis of disjunctions in the size of structures, the existence of concentric barriers of structures of different function (residential, commercial, etc.), changes in grid orientation, size and manners of approach to individual units, height of structures, and so forth.

In short, the amount of variation above the level of the cell, matrix and structure may be very great both within a corpus and between corpora. In other words, architectonic codes are highly creative in terms of the amount of variation in the arrangement of significative units, even within the same settlement. Nevertheless, characteristic patterns of arrangement of units appear to occur for each code, and we may say that there evidently exist various kinds of rules of formation which prescribe formative organizations recognizable to members of a society as belonging to that code as permissable variations on a theme.

In certain cases, large-scale formative patterns may achieve canonical "idiomaticization" in a manner analogous to the rules of formation which prescribe the organization of the type of architectonic sign termed above a *matrix*[a] of cells. A grid of streets is essentially a *diagram* of relational organization of structures and groups of structures (blocks, neighborhoods), a prescription of significantly-appropriate relationships.

In other words, the architectonic sign is an increasingly more abstract or *diagrammatic* entity the "higher" one goes "above" the level of the space-cell, consisting of sets of syntactic rules of combination of significative entities like cells or more or less "fixed" cell-patterns or matrices. If we take an "architectonic code" as meaning, among other things, sets of elemental units, relationships among those units, and rules governing relationships, then a code may be considered as *storing* certain kinds of information both overtly (as in the case of the range of permissable space-cells) and implicitly (as in the case of larger-scale entities such as matrices, structures, neighborhoods, grids, and so forth).

But there will most likely be a kind of overlap between overt and implicitly-coded information—as in the case of certain characteristic cell-matrices, which (to make a direct analogy with language) are partially reminiscent of idiomatic phrasings in speech. It would appear to be the case, as our Minoan and Egyptian examples illustrate, that idiomaticization is a characteristic feature of formative organization: it is the case both with a verbal idiom ("he blew his stack") and an architectonic matrix (a Hall System) that the constitutive elements in each occur singly in other contexts with varying significance—"he blew his stack" : "he blew his nose" :: Minoan cell (a)+(b)+(c) : (a) in another context (where it serves simply as a light well in any number of other contextual sequences).

What is "stored" as such in an architectonic code, then, are (1) entities which are directly significative, such as space-cells, which are associated with certain parameters of meaning or function, and (2) entities which comprise diagrams of interrelationship among significative elements—our matrices, structures, grids and so forth. It will be clear that "idiomaticization" or pattern-fixing may occur at various levels of organization above the level of the space-cell. In a given corpus, for example, matrices and structures may be more or less permanently "fixed" so that only one or two or several building-types recur constantly with a more or less fixed format. In some corpora, as for example the Minoan, the format of structures of residential function exhibit a wide degree of variation: no two Minoan houses are identical in formation.

The systematic collation of formations across corpora has barely begun, despite a plethora of impressionistic accounts, and we have a great deal to learn about the apparent "universality" of formative types. Nevertheless, *architectonic universals only exist in code-specific situations*, and are consequently subject to a wide range of contextual variation.

If it is in fact the case that the space-cell occupies a privileged position in a corpus by being coded or stored as such, what of its constituent "parts"? We are accustomed to consider cellular formations as made up of component entities such as walls, floors, ceilings, doors, stairwells, windows, and the like. But is it the case that the space-cell, as an architectonic *sign*, is "made up of" other signs?

We will be concerned here with several issues: first, the question of the singularity of reference of such entities; secondly, the question of the contrastive identity of these entities (i.e., do such entities all "blend into" one another or are they discrete elements in a code?); thirdly, with the relationship of such items with aspects of material realization and its evident variability; and fourthly, with the specific roles of such items in the definition and delimitation of space-cells themselves.

Clearly, these issues are closely interrelated and cannot be neatly separated, so that a conclusion proposed for one question will have important ramifications for each of the others.

Preliminary to a consideration of these issues is the question of the recognition and identity of subcellular entities. On this score there is a good deal of confusion introduced by the problem of the *material* variability of formations. Are a blue wall and a red wall which are formally identical on other counts (size, shape, material composition, position in a space-cell, etc.) in fact "different" entities?

The question cannot be answered properly outside the context of a given corpus. It may be the case that in corpus (Q) such a material difference is associated with different *signata* (e.g., contrasts in social status or function, aesthetic associations, etc.), whereas in corpus (Q') no such significative difference is evident—i.e., the choice of wall coloration may be dependent upon arbitrary and dynamically-changing extra-architectonic factors.

It is evident that such significative distinctions as suggested for corpus (Q) comprise a realm of signification categorically different from that suggested above for formal (geometric) signification; we will return to this issue below.

In concert with our discussion above, it is proposed that an architectonic array achieves definition and identity by means of perceptually palpable disjunctions in formation (e.g., boundary conditions described, through edges, by changes in orientation and alignment within the array. It was suggested that disjunctions in formation will generally be considered as being correlative (in *various* senses, as is now apparent) to disjunctive contrasts in signification.

Subcellular entities achieve discriminative identity through contrastive opposition to other such entities. A wall is distinguished from a floor, or a doorway, on the basis of the presence or absence of certain *features* of formation. Thus, a given item such as (a) (below) contrasts with (b) on the basis of contrastive features of relative height, length and width. Indeed, it is clearly the case that such formations are distinguishable on the basis of the application to an array of a generalized analytic reference frame with three coordinate parameters so that in a general sense, (a) : (b) :: (h = 1 $\gg$ w) : (h $\ll$ 1 = w). ("$\gg$ " = very much greater than).

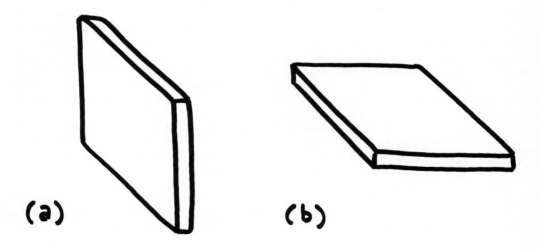

(a)   (b)

The situation is compounded, however, by the obvious fact that items such as either (a) or (b) may exhibit a great deal of variation in relative proportions, or at least apparently so. Thus, compare (a) and (a') below:

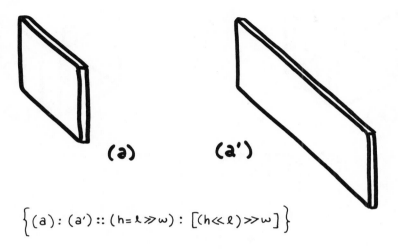

$$\left\{ (a): (a') :: (h = \ell \gg w) : \left[(h \ll \ell) \gg w \right] \right\}$$

Such a situation would appear to throw the issue of formative organization into the bottomless bin of non-discrete, gradient formation in which the analyst would seem to have to choose between admitting into a typology of formations a large set of form-classes with a few ranges of proportional variation in each, or a single set within which there occur a wide variety of gradient transformations.

But the problem is in fact one of focus and perspective, and it will be clear that we can speak of such "entities" in a very limited sense *out of context.*

If we understand such formations as being purposeful principally in the sense of their role as discriminators of space-cells, then much of the aforementioned problem dissolves, since it will be primarily their *relational* aspect as elements in an array which will distinguish them in a code. From such a perspective, variations in internal relative proportions within formations (a) and (b), including the kind of variation suggested by the last example ((a) vs. (a')), will be patently secondary to their opposition *to each other.*

Consequently, a range or *parameter of variation* in items of the type (a) will be contrastively opposed to an equivalent situation in (b).

In other words, the significance of such subcellular entities lies in their *opposition* to other equivalent entities; as architectonic *signs* they have a principal function in *discriminating one space-cell from another.* They comprise, in effect, tools to make tools, the latter being directly significative, the former being indirectly significative (or rather significative in the sense of cueing perception of directly-significative formations).

Thus, in the following example, space-cells (A) and (B) are distinguished on the basis of a perceptually-palpable opposition between two subcellular entities (x) and (y):

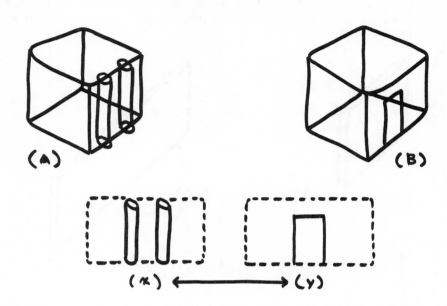

Similarly, the following space-cells (C) and (D) are distinguished on the basis of another binary opposition, in this case between formations (v) and (w):

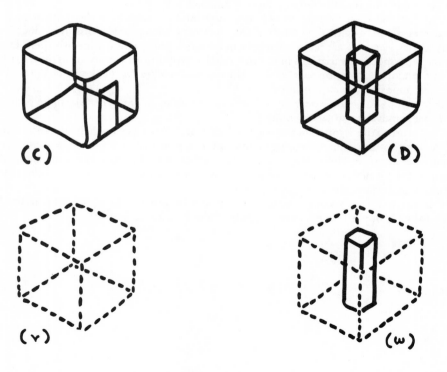

The space-cell is composed of sense-discriminative formations which as signs are primarily significative in terms of their contrastive oppositions to other such signs. In and of themselves, they lack singularity of reference; they are arbitrary, conventional, and code-specific units which are significant in terms of the architectonic code itself: they are *systemically* significant.

The situation, however, is complicated by the fact that in a given code, certain formal configurations *may* in fact have a singularity of reference in addition to their systemic function. This phenomenon, termed elsewhere by the writer *sematectonic*[a] meaning, will be discussed below,[2] touching as it does on the important problem of architectonic symbolism. For the moment we are concerned with their primary role as systemic sign-formations.

We have now in a sense come full circle to the issue addressed at the beginning of Chapter II above, namely the question of the generalized array. It should now be apparent that the process of defining and identifying systemic signs in a particular code is an inevitable correlate of such a process.

We will make a stronger claim, however: namely that because of their role as discriminators of cellular formation, only those entities which participate in contrastive oppositions to other such entities in equivalent contexts will be admitted to the repertory of systemic signs in a given corpus. Such a criterion will allow us to differentiate systemic signs from their contextual variants.[a]

A given item will be admitted as a constituent systemic unit in a given corpus insofar as it stands in opposition to other such units in a space-cell. Thus, item (a) below will be opposed to items (b), (c), (d), (e), etc.:

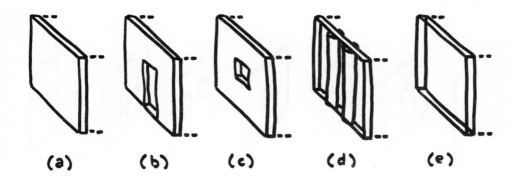

(a)   (b)   (c)   (d)   (e)

just as item (f) in the following will be successively opposed to (g) and (h):

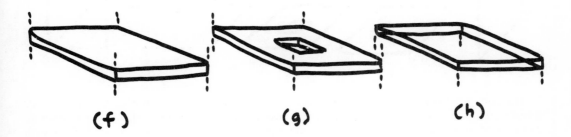

(f)   (g)   (h)

The identity of systemic signs will be *code-specific*, and will provide us with yet another means for the comparison of architectonic corpora. In corpus (R), for example, the system of such signs may comprise the following:

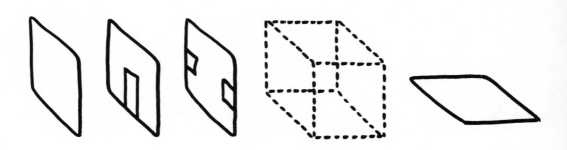

which will contrast with that of corpus (R'):

The system of subcellular formations will vary from one corpus to another, often to a very great degree (note that we are not considering material variation, which will add yet another dimension of potential contrast). Some systems will be relatively "simple" in comparison with others—i.e., in the sense of having fewer systemic signs.

Clearly, however, there is no justification for distinguishing one corpus from another in a qualitative sense, if that distinction is based on the number of systemic items in a subcellular system (i.e., "simpler" systems are not more "primitive" than those which have a larger number of such units). It should be apparent that simplicity or complexity is a function of perspective on the code or the level of organization being addressed: code (S), with a relatively small number of systemic units, may exhibit a wide and rich range of contextual variation both materially and syntactically (i.e., in terms of the parameters of cell-matrix aggregation), while code (S'), with a relatively large number of such units, may exhibit fewer material and syntactic variations.[3]

Nor is there the slightest justification for equating formal simplicity or complexity with level of complexity of culture in general. This point has been made strongly and adequately by others in other areas of inquiry, and needs no additional comment here.[4]

The following chart illustrates the set of systemic *forms* established on the basis of contrastive oppositions observable in the exemplary corpus of formations discussed above.

minoan				
	FORM		MASS	SPACE
A			+	−
B			+	−
C		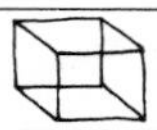 (1:1:1)	−	+
D			+	+
E			+	+
F			−	+
G			+	+
H			+	+
I		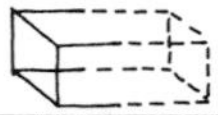 (1:1:1+)	−	+
J		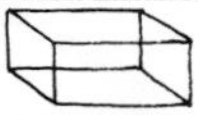 (1:2:3)	−	+
K			+	−
L			+	−
M			+	−
N			−	+

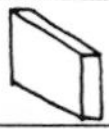

Figure 4

The chart exhibits a number of salient features which deserve comment here. The first is that these units (let us henceforth refer to them as systemic *forms*)[a] are specified materially as belonging to two distinctive classes (*viz.*, those occurring as mass-formations, and those occurring in the corpus as spatial or volumnar formations). In addition, several *forms* occur both in space and in mass (D,E,G,H), depending upon their contextual position in a space-cell.

Secondly, the number of *forms* is quite limited, about a score. In other words, the number of *forms* is *not un*limited: the enormous variation in cellular and material formation in the corpus arises out of the interactive and contextual combination, reduplication, embedding, and transformation of these few units in the code. The productivity or creativity of an architectonic code, and its seemingly transfinite possible formations, rests upon the interactive relationship of such *forms*.

Two additional points are worthy of note in this regard. First, the rules of combination of *forms* are corpus-specific. Thus, the above corpus admits (1) below, but does not permit (2):

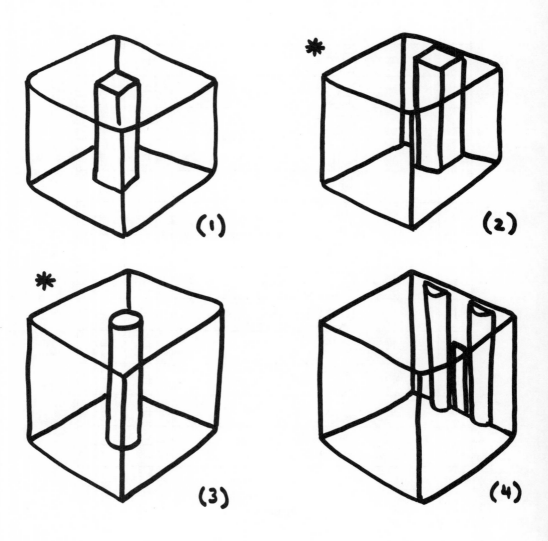

On the other hand, the corpus does *not* admit (3) above, but does permit (4). Evidently, a corpus will reveal, in its structural oppositions, certain *asymmetries* of realization: homologies which might be expected by the analyst may not form part of a given code.

Consequently an analysis will seek to establish not only what may occur (be realized) in a corpus, but also what it appears to forbid at a given time and place. In addition, it may be found that in certain contrastive oppositions, one term of the opposition may occur with great frequency whereas the other term may occur relatively rarely. Thus the latter may be seen as a highly "marked" formation in the sense that its occurrence is a special, or focused-upon event, calling attention to itself by its unusual occurrence. In the case of (3) above, it may be unattested as a formation because of the accidents of survival in the archaeological record. Should this be the case, then the latter type of marked-unmarked opposition would be present.

In other words, just as a corpus will specify certain formations as canonical or acceptable, it will proscribe others. There exist, in other words, *semiotic constraints*[a] in an architectonic code.

The second point of interest, in a sense correlative to the previous, is the fact that not all possible ranges of formal variation will occur in a given corpus. This may be seen by referring to the chart in Figure 4 above, where, for example, *form* /C/ only occurs as a space-formation and not as a mass-formation; there *will* be corpora where the latter possibility is fulfilled.

Clearly, architectonic masses and spaces are in no way analogous to the sounds and silences of language, for example; architectonic spaces are not "empty" of signification (even though masses may carry more highly articulated information, this is not a "presence/absence" situation but a "more *vs.* less" situation). The system is highly marked and asymmetrical.

The point cannot be overly stressed that architectonic spaces are significant in systemic (and in some cases sematectonic) ways *independently* of the presence or absence of correlative lexico-semantic items in the language of members of a given society.

There may, however, be a salient homology between the architectonic and linguistic codes with respect to a trait of "alternative patterning," comprising in the former the universally-employed framework of mass/space sequencing, and, in the latter, the consonantal/vocalic alternative sequencing (similarly universal) or "syllabic" framework.

This alternative patterning is realized differently in the two codes in the sense that in language it is unilinearly syntagmatic or sequential, whereas in architecture it is *tridimensionally syntagmatic*, involving both linear sequencing and consecutive embeddings.

The existence of the mass/space alternation in the architectonic code points up the evident fact that *forms* are themselves classifiable in terms of certain manifest features: the set of *forms* is thereby bifurcated into two subsets. In addition, it has been noted that several *forms* may function either spatially or massively, depending upon the cellular context and, consequently, upon their positional contiguity or separation from one another.

Note that in an architectonic system, a contiguity of two space-*forms* yields a larger space of compounded configuration: the contrast between two such *forms*, then, would appear to be "neutralized" and the forms merged or blended. While it is evidently the case that such a "neutralization" may remain unmarked in a given array, it is clear that corpora in general tend to preserve the contrastive opposition in *some* way—for example by distinctions in material articulation (framing of a doorway or window, for example, or with a variety of other articulations).[5]

The situation, in other words, tends toward the preservation of discrete oppositions where the syntagmatic patterning of *forms* is concerned, and this is noticeable not only in the case of alternative (mass/space) patterning, but also in the case of *form* sequencing involving juxtapositions of mass/mass or space/space. Once again it is important to recall that an architectonic code is addressed to the mechanisms of human visual perception, which serve to distinguish entities on the basis of formational disjunctions cued by boundary conditions (edges), contrastive oppositions in textural medium or in color, size, and so forth. An architectonic system uses any means at its disposal to get its messages across.

The existence of two overlapping subsets in the set of *forms* specific to our corpus raises the question as to the extent that we may be dealing with not merely a taxonomy of individual *forms*, but rather a *system of forms*.

In the list of *forms* given in Figure 4 above, it will be seen that such entities are distinguished from one another on the basis of their geometric properties. Thus, *form* /D/ is opposed to /E/ in the following way:

$$\text{/D/} : \text{/E/} :: (h \ll 1, w) : (h, 1 \gg w)$$

Similarly,

$$\text{/A/} : \text{/B/} :: (h \gg (1{=}w)) : (h \gg \text{diam.})$$

Also,

$$\text{/C/} : \text{/J/} :: (h{=}1{=}w) : (1h{:}21{:}3w)$$
$$\text{/C/} : \text{/I/} :: (h{=}1{=}w) : ((h{=}1) < w)$$

and so forth.

In other words, the differences among *forms* in a system of *forms* comprise relative ratios in internal proportion, and all such units can be compared on a common set of tridimensional co-ordinates. In this way, the various *forms* specific to a corpus will be seen to occupy relative contrastive positions in a coordinate space. This, of course, is code-specific: not all contrasts may be significative in the same ways.

It would appear that we have two different ways of classifying *forms*—one, on the basis of their inherent or internal geometric features, and a second, on the basis of a bipartite categorization according to medium-type (not specific materials). The question arises, however, as to the extent to which the latter classification is ambiguous.

It has already been noted that the mass/space opposition appears to be related to certain properties of geometric formation itself—namely, some aspect of relative positioning of *forms*. Looked at in this manner, it will become evident that the media opposition is in some way secondary, for some *forms* occupy positions peripheral to others, while some occupy infixed or embedded positions within others. The following subsystems are revealed:

1. peripheral forms: /A/B/D/E/F/G/H/K/L/M/
2. embedded forms: /B/C/I/J/N/A
3. central forms: /A/B/F/G/H/

Some *forms* may be both peripheral and central, viz., /A/B/F/G/H/, while others may be both central and embedded, viz., /A/B/. The frame of reference of these relational terms, of course, is the space-cell itself.

In other words, it is the case that certain *forms* may have more than one distinguishing geometric feature. Thus, /A/ has a property of embeddedness, peripherality and centrality, whereas *form* /F/ has centrality and peripherality. /A/ is distinguished from /B/ in context /C/ in that only the former has centrality. This is illustrated in the following:

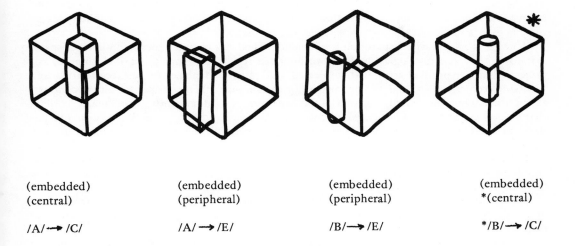

| (embedded) | (embedded) | (embedded) | (embedded) |
| (central) | (peripheral) | (peripheral) | *(central) |

| /A/ → /C/ | /A/ → /E/ | /B/ → /E/ | */B/ → /C/ |

(The corpus manifests an asymmetry of realizations; even though /B/ → /C/ looks as though it might be a simple homology to /A/ → /C/, it does not occur.)

Form /B/, however, does manifest a property of centrality, but only as infixed in *forms* /I/ and /J/, and then only when reduplicated (in which case it may alternate with /A/).

The property of peripherality, however, is ambiguous, and we need to distinguish between *lateral* peripherality (right/left/front/back) and *vertical* peripherality (up/down), since the two properties will be associated with different *forms*.

Thus, /D/, /H/, /K/ have a property of lateral peripherality, which serves to distinguish them from /E/, /F/, /G/, and /L/. In the case of /L/, however, any contrast between the axes of lateral peripherality (right/left/front/back) is in a sense "neutralized"; /L/ is consequently one single surface. With *form* /M/, however, a further degree of "neutralization" occurs: /M/ = /L/ minus one vertical peripheral axis (up or "above").

It will be evident that the sextuply-contrastive "axes" referred to here are isomorphic to the generalized frame of reference employed here and elsewhere, as well as to the tripartite binary contrastive axes of the human form, conceived as projecting, through its bilateral symmetries and contrasts, "front" vs. "back," "right" vs. "left," "above" vs. "below," and, generically, "center" vs. "periphery." Of these contrastive somatic axes, only "right" and "left" are mirror-reversals; in the other cases, the two terms of the opposition are formatively different.

This situation has many cultural resonances, notably in the culture-specific semantic "weightings" or markings given the various opposed terms (cf. the generically positive weighting of up/above, front, and right vs. the negative weighting of down/below, back, and left in many societies).

Ultimately, it would seem, both our generalized reference frame and, perhaps, the generic structure of the components of built environments themselves are founded on palpable constancies of human *somatotopy*[a].[6] It may be tempting to regard the structure of the architectonic code, in its fundamental "logic," as a generalization of the inherent relationships of the human body as an instrument in the measurement of the world.

Such would hold whether or not corpora were predominantly rectilinear or curvilinear in realization, for obvious transformational reasons. It might appear to be the case that there is an inherent "six-sidedness" in our (geometric) perception of objects of any kind (i.e., a tripartite set of binary contrasts), if we were to follow the suggestions of G. A. Miller and P. N. Johnson-Laird (1976) in their recent provocative study.[7]

But of course such a geometric logic of formation is necessarily *equilibrated* in the mature adult, as studies by Piaget and many others have demonstrated, with *topological* and *perspectival* reference systems in perception.[8] The three sets of spatial concepts appear to be acquired sequentially in early childhood (topological, perspectival, geometric).

Hence it is evident that a space-cell is to be understood as a complex formation in three space-manifolds:[a] (1) as a topological 'unicum' or bounded region with some kind of closure; (2) as a projective or perspectival array with projected and contrasted planes or surfaces relative to a (shiftable) centrality; (3) and as a geometric formation with inherent tripartite binary contrasts as specified above. Necessarily, since it is the case even in predominantly "curvilinear" corpora that objects are aligned and oriented relative to each other as well as internally, we would be justified in speaking of a perceptual "neutralization" of certain geometric distinctions or disjunctions.[9]

The result is a concise and systematic picture of the organization of architectonic *forms* as composed of bundles of relationally-defined features whose function is to discriminate one *form* from another.

The nature of the architectonic *form*, then, is not that of a primitive or ultimate constituent in a code, but of a formal systemic unit itself composed of simultaneously-occurring *distinctive features*. Each *form* manifests two or more such relational features.

In a sense this situation is analogous to that obtaining in the relationship between forms and space-cells, wherein *forms* have a systemic significance in distinguishing *cells* from each other: geometric *features*[a] are similarly significant in a systemic sense in serving to distinguish one *form* from another.

In contrast to *forms,* which occur (except for situations of "neutralization" described above) in *contiguity* and tridimensional sequence, distinctive *features* occur *simultaneously,* serving, in their interactive copresence, to define and delimit individual *forms* with respect to one another. The situation is apparently homologous to that in language codes, wherein phonemic units occur on a sequential or syntagmatic axis, or axis of copresent combinations, while the bundles of distinctive features (which as signs serve to distinguish one phoneme from another) occupy a paradigmatic axis, or axis of simultaneity.

The system of distinctive features in the architectonic code reveals a series of increasingly finer distinctions. Thus, the system exhibits a contrast between what we may term "inherent" and "compositional" features. The former involves "internal" relationships of *forms,* whereas the latter involve "external" relationships between *forms* (within the overall framework of the cell). Bifurcating both subsystems is the distinction between mass and space realization: several *forms* (/D/E/F/G/H/) have alternative realization depending on context. *Form* /G/ may be realized spatially (as a central-infixing in peripheral *form* /E/) or massively (as a central-embedding in itself-in-space).

Consequently, each *form* comprises a *bundle* of at least two *features.* Geometric features, as noted above, serve principally to discriminate architectonic *forms,* and are thereby systemically significant. They are, in other words, sense-discriminative in nature (as are *forms* themselves with respect to *cells*).

This situation is compounded by the fact that in certain instances both *forms* and *features* may simultaneously serve in a *sense-determinative*[a] fashion—i.e., with singularity of denotation[a] (vs. their other role in "double articulation"). *Forms* /G/ and /H/, for example, are not only systemically significant, they are also metonymically indicative of juncture or connection or intersection between cells. Others (e.g., /D/, /F/, as spatially-realized) signify *visual* connectivity among cells.

Note that a necessary property common to all these *forms* is *peripherality.* Hence, from a *feature* point of view, peripherality is singularly denotative of juncture or intersection. But different peripheral *forms* provide distinctive information. For example, /E/ provides information about intersection with another or other cells, but is not indicative of connection (only contiguity). /E/ with /G/ infixed provides information about *both* contiguity and connectivity. Some corpora will provide a further distinction between a *form* of the type /G/ $\longrightarrow$ /E/ which provides information about connectivity within a structure in contrast to connectivity between structures, and so forth. In such a case, the latter *may not* be distinctive formally but rather materially (as when a doorway is heavily articulated in outline).[10]

Singularity of denotation among systemic signs such as *forms* and *features*, what we termed before "sematectonic" signification, involves a number of different functions.

For example, a *feature* may function *configuratively* in signalling divisions of a formation into formal units of varying complexity. Peripherality, then, is *both* systemic and configurative.

A *form* may function *redundantly,* as when it focuses upon another distinct form so as to enhance or augment its occurrence (for example the use of engaged columns adjacent to a certain doorway in a structure, contrasting with other doorways without engaged columns, or doorways with smaller engaged columns, etc.; in such a case, the *form* serves to enhance the perceptual attention to that door). A *feature* may function redundantly in the case of the aforementioned, where a given formation is augmented or perceptually enhanced by a scalar emphasis on one or more dimensions (e.g., the doorway is taller than the others, or wider, or deeper).

Forms and *features* may also be used *expressively* in exhibiting the "trademark" of a certain builder through certain distortions of scale, etc., or in the emphasis of certain significative formations at the expense of the diminution of others.

In contrast to systemic significance, sematectonic significance (particularly with respect to its expressive functions) is not necessarily organized in binary fashion but may be scalar or graded in some way such that distinctions in expressive content are associated or correlated with gradations in formation.

The functions listed above clearly do not exhaust the possibilities (see below, Chapter IV); they are intended to be illustrative of some of the multiplicity of functions exhibited by architectonic signs. The nature of architectonic semiosis is only beginning to be understood in a systematic way, and an enormous amount of work on large bodies of synchronic data awaits our attention.

Before passing on to our final, concluding section, another point regarding architectonic distinctive features is worthy of comment. It may in fact be the case that a comparison with language here is even more apt than suggested above, for it is becoming apparent that both the existence and internal ordering of the system of distinctive features finds independent confirmation in certain behavioral properties of the human perceptual system, particularly regarding the manner whereby the child gradually comes to assimilate and acquire spatial and object concepts. Work in perceptual and cognitive psychology in recent years has found increasing evidence for the sequential acquisition of various classes of spatial features which achieve systematic and equilibrated relative oppositions in the architectonic code.[11]

In other words, what is distinguished in the set of copresent features in the code is acquired *separately,* in tandem.

Understanding of the relationship between the acquisition of architectonic and linguistic distinctive features is still largely in its infancy. But there is some indication of homologous *processes* in the acquisition of features of both codes; it is not clear to what extent it may be possible to speak of equivalent formations in both systems. Certainly the latter is not required by the theory of architectonic systems elaborated here.

Our primary point here is that just as the existence of the code-specific system of linguistic distinctive features,—proposed by N. Troubetzkoy to, and brought to its full picture by R. Jakobson and others (Jakobson and Waugh, 1978)[12]—is confirmed by the study of language acquisition in children (and its reversed, piecemeal formational loss through aphasia), so the existence of the system of architectonic features may now find independent confirmation in comparable study of spatial and object concept-acquisition and representation.

For a fuller discussion of this complicated issue the reader is referred to the work of Bower, and Moore (1976) confirming the acquisition of "compositional" features of object-arrays *separately* and *prior to* the acquisition of internal or "inherent" features of forms themselves; and the studies by J. Goodnow and others (Goodnow, 1977) indicating that children, in acquiring drawing skills, progress through the assimilation of one feature to another, incorporating and equilibrating features into a systematic whole.[13]

Our description of architectonic forms has focused principally on *geometric* or tridimensional signs. Generations of analysts have been accustomed to speak of surfaces, planes, facades, elevations, and so forth, as significant formations in their own right. The question which arises here concerns the systemic position of such "entities" in the system of formations elaborated here.

The question is pertinent in the present framework for it would appear to be the case that in some sense, planes or surfaces "coexist" with (tridimensional) *forms* as similarly serving to discriminate one space-cell from another, or one matrix or structure from others. Looked at from this perspective, it seems to be the case that cellular *forms* can be simultaneously two-dimensional planes and near surfaces of three-dimensional *forms* (or sets of forms).

Consider that the interior "surface" of a rectilinear cell consists of six planes, corresponding to the set of six planar intersections of the binary-contrasted axes of front vs. back, right vs. left, and top vs. bottom; in other words:

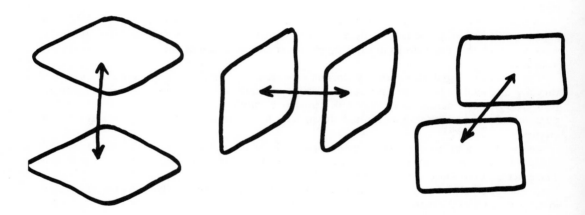

Consider further that such planes are copresent with the tridimensional *forms* which serve to distinguish one cell from another, and that in fact they provide *additional* information (or, rather, information of a different kind) regarding such discriminations *not* provided by the set of *forms* —namely, perspectival and directional position.

Forms /D/ and /E/, for example, carry only configurative or geometric information, and are not specified in terms of their direction or orientation. That is, /D/ is unspecified as to whether it occupies either the "top" or "bottom" of a cell space (i.e., of central *form* /C/, etc.), it is only specified as to its generic vertical peripherality. Is it necessary, then, to propose the existence of two /D/s? Or to propose, by analogy, four /E/s? Clearly not, since we are concerned principally with geometric or formal information.

Conversely, a *plane*[a] can be conceived as carrying no unambiguous specific information regarding the kinds of *form*-relationships evident, say, in the following:

where one or more *forms* are relationally-embedded in another one. Here we are dealing with two different *forms*; from a *planar* perspective, however, such compound formations are identical or equivalent. On the other hand, in the following case:

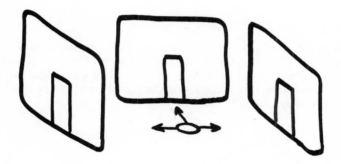

we are dealing with three different *planes* but three identical *forms*.

In addition, it will be the case that *planes* are not necessarily *coterminous* with single peripheral *forms*, as in the case of a uniform facade of a multicellular structure:[14]

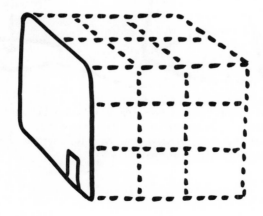

Hence it is clear that with *planes* and *forms* we are dealing with two different *perspectives* on cellular and architectonic formation, both of which may be seen as contributing to the sense-discrimination of cells, and of cell-aggregates (matrices, structures, etc.). It will be evident that *planes* also serve sense-determinative roles in a code—as, for example in corpora where different types of facades are indicative of differently-functional aggregations of cells: e.g., highly articulated planar facades = public buildings, etc.

It appears to be the case that *planes* and *forms*, as signs, carry partly-complementary and partly-redundant systemic information regarding the distinction of one cell from another. If we picture the various perspectives on significant formations in an architectonic code as outlined above (viz., features, forms, cells, matrices, etc.), as hierarchical "levels" of organization, then a planar perspective cannot be admitted into such a conceptual space "between," say, *features* and *forms,* or "between" *forms* and *cells,* but must be admitted as a "parallel" level of organization to that of *forms.* In other words,

  (1) .features
  (2) . . . . .forms. . . . . . .planes
  (3) . . . .(alt. patterning)
  (4) .cells
  (5) . . . . .matrices
  (6) . . . . structures
  (n) . . . . (etc.)

It need not be emphasized that just as *forms* are code-specific in their detailed properties or features, so also will *planes* be specific to a given corpus. Corpus (T), with a rectilinear organization, may distinguish planar formation by means of a sextuple system of features, whereas corpus (T'), with a curvilinear organization, may distinguish planar formation by means of a binary system of features, as suggested by the following:

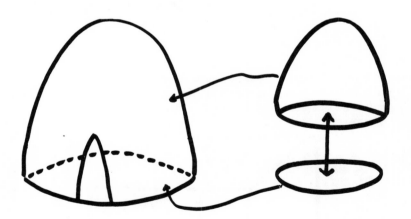

From the point of view of corpus (T), however, corpus (T') may be said to manifest a "neutralization" of portions of a six-fold distinctive contrast (and vice-versa).

Many corpora are, from this point of view, "mixed"—for example the Minoan, with sextuple, ternary and binary subsystems of planar formation:

If the *forms* of a code are organized into a system on the basis of composite realization of bundles of *features*, then it will be evident that *planes* similarly reveal a parallel and complementary system of features:

$$\left\{ \begin{array}{c} \text{ABOVE} \\ \updownarrow \\ \text{BELOW} \end{array} \right\} \longleftrightarrow \left\{ \begin{array}{c} \text{BEFORE} \\ \updownarrow \\ \text{BEHIND} \end{array} \right\} \longleftrightarrow \left\{ \begin{array}{c} \text{RIGHT} \\ \updownarrow \\ \text{LEFT} \end{array} \right\}$$

Consequently, the system of *features* defining *forms* is modified from what was presented above to the following:

$$\left\{ \begin{array}{c} \text{VERTICAL} \rightleftharpoons \text{LATERAL} \\ \updownarrow \\ \text{EMBEDDED} \rightleftharpoons \text{NON-EMBEDDED} \end{array} \right\} \xleftrightarrow{\text{PERIPHERAL}\quad\text{CENTRAL}} \left\{ \begin{array}{c} \text{EMBEDDED} \\ \updownarrow \\ \text{NON-EMBEDDED} \end{array} \right\}$$

—which, moreover, is in line with our initial proposals. It will be clear that our "finer distinctions" (see above) properly belong to the system of *planar* features.

Hence our portrayal of the various "levels" of organization of the significant formations of a code will be modified on the first two "levels":

features	features
forms	planes

Regarding the situation where a *plane* serves to define and delimit an *aggregate* of cells, as in a uniform "facade" of a structure:

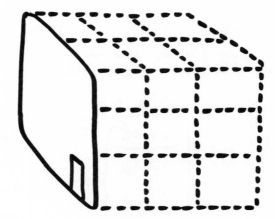

from the perspective elaborated here such a situation may be seen as a process of neutralization of the following:

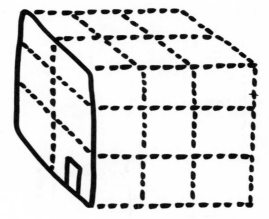

Architectonic systems, as noted above in another context, tend toward the preservation of contrastive oppositions in a variety of ways—indeed, in any way possible—so that it will *normally* be the case that cellular discriminations are cued in some way, whether through material articulation:

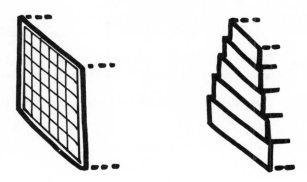

which in various ways will either (or also) be signalled by the presence of peripheral/embedded *forms:*

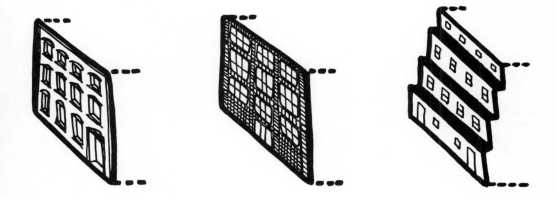

The latter situation appears to be generally the case in corpora, whereas situations where a single, blank *plane* serves to define an entire cell-aggregate vertically-stacked tend to be rarer (and hence, in a given corpus, perhaps more highly "marked").

In a parallel fashion, it is necessary to incorporate the third space-manifold into our picture of formal organization, namely *topological* features. Once again, the notion of the space-cell as a topological unicum has been implicit in our description from the outset (see above, Chapter II). From a topological point of view, the cell is defined as a formation with a property of boundedness; it is, in other words, a *domain*. Our picture of the organization of an architectonic code necessarily requires the incorporation of topological signs, which serve a sense-discriminative function vis-a-vis cells. As an entity in the code, *domain* is itself composed of copresent *features* which serve to distinguish *domains*.

Topologically, we recognize the existence of binary contrastive oppositions between boundedness vs. unboundedness, and inside vs. outside, both (again) relative terms.

Similar to the situation of *planes* above, boundary conditions may delimit or distinguish cells, matrices (as with functionally-distinct "zones" of a structure), neighborhoods and settlements. An entire settlement may comprise a topological unicum *in contrast to* other settlements; once again we may conceive of such a unicum as resulting from various kinds of neutralization of multiple bounded unicums, parallel to the processes described above for *forms* and *planes.*

From a topological perspective, distinctions in either *planar* or *formal* formation become neutralized or non-relevant, just as from a *planar* perspective various disjunctions in *form* will be non-relevant.

Such a picture is in accord with the general notion of invariance behind variability, or relational invariance, seen above as constituting one of the fundamental principles of architectonic organization.

The resultant picture of the organization of the architectonic code, if that is portrayed by means of "levels," is as follows:

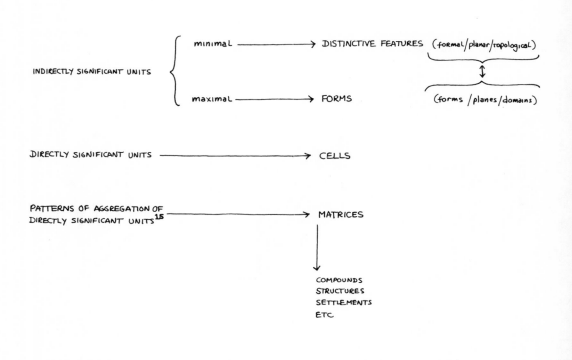

It will be clear that the multidimensional nature of built environments requires a *multiple contribution* to the definition of cells and other directly significant formations or patterns of formation, a situation in obvious and necessary contrast to what obtains in other semiotic systems (e.g., language and language-based codes). Once again, the nature of the processes of perceptual address, and their resultant mechanisms, serve to contrast architectonic and linguistic semiosis.

A word of caution is required here regarding the nature of the representation of architectonic organization biased by the limitations of the written word. It cannot be emphasized strongly enough that we are dealing here with a multidimensional, relational organization which is not reducible to the graphic "levels" in the model shown above. Such "levels" should not be taken too literally as hard-and-fast and strongly-disjunctive plateaux in a hierarchy. We are dealing in fact with a variety of different *perspectives* on synchronous objects such that the identity and delimitation of any one "entity" is modified by the copresence of all others in a network of relations, in the variety of ways suggested in our account. This has been implicit from the outset of our discussion. It should be clear also that the nature of architectonic signification is itself highly complex and multidimensional: our example of the Minoan Hall System has suggested that a complex architectonic *sign* is a *composite realization* of a variety of significant formations whose code-specific interrelationships do not at all resemble an aggregate of building blocks, but rather describe a multidimensional semantic domain whose "component parts" are drawn from a highly disparate set of entities, some of which are redundant, complementary, and even in certain instances contradictory.

Moreover, such a formation is itself a modal component in a multimodal behavioral situation whose various component formations are interactively equilibrated in extremely complex ways, beyond our present abilities to characterize systematically. Although any semiotic system has its own coherences and internally-consistent (albeit asymmetrical and highly marked) formations, in daily life everything is intertwined like galaxies passing through each other: what we weave in the ordering of our dynamically-unfolding personal and societal realities is composed of highly disparate and continually changing materials, and we are continually changing instruments, sometimes using one alone, but mostly balancing several in parallel or in tandem. What is begun in one thread (language) is completed in another (spatial relations), only to be modified by other considerations at a moment's notice.[16] A boundary between two settlements may be a city wall or a piece of legislation, a disjunction in building materials or in dialect, a river or a proscription on who may marry whom, a difference in religion or a railway line.

FOOTNOTES

CHAPTER III

[1] J. Hardoy, *Precolumbian Cities,* New York, 1973, 380 ff.

[2] See below, Chapter IV.

[3] There are evident parallels here with the phonological systems of verbal language wherein systems with fewer phonemic units allow of wider contextual variations than those with a greater number of phonemes.

[4] See Preziosi, *Origins . . . ,* Chapter IV, for the problem of the 'technological fallacy.'

[5] This question is the subject of a monograph currently being prepared by the writer on environmental perception.

[6] On somatotopy or the significant use of the body and body parts in space, see Preziosi, 1978k.

[7] G. A. Miller and P. N. Johnson-Laird, *Language and Perception,* New York, 1976.

[8] See J. Piaget and B. Inhelder, *The Child's Conception of Space,* New York, 1967; J. Piaget, *Genetic Epistemology,* New York, 1970.

[9] See Preziosi, *Origins . . . ,* Chapter IV.

[10] In the Minoan system, for example, little if any distinctions in size and configuration exist between interior doorways and exterior doorways. The decoding of such information will depend on other formative features. This is in contrast with some other corpora, such as the Egyptian, where building entrances are very heavily 'marked' in terms of size, centrality of position in a facade, strong material articulation, and so forth.

[11] On this question, see now J. Goodnow, *Children Drawing,* Cambridge, Mass., 1977.

[12] R. Jakobson and L. R. Waugh, *The Sound Shape of Language,* Bloomington, Indiana, 1979 (forthcoming).

[13] See T. G. R. Bower, *The Perceptual World of the Child,* Cambridge, Mass., 1977, Chapter 7; and M. K. Moore, "Object Permanence and Object Identity: a Stage Developmental Model," paper presented to the Society for Research in Child Development, Denver, April 1975.

[14] In addition, it will be evident that the reverse obtains, namely where more than one *plane* is coterminous with a single *form.*

[15] Except, of course, for 'idiomatic' or relatively fixed patterns, as noted above in connection with the Minoan hall system (Chapter II).

[16] Discussed further in the Appendix below.

Chapter IV
Architectonic Meaning

INTRODUCTION

The study of architectonic meaningfulness is a mare's nest of conflicting opinion, and the student of the built environment is normally at a loss to construct a coherent and holistic picture of the situation. Generations of studies have, if anything, one thing in common—an agreement that the situation is extraordinarily complex. There are evidently so many senses in which architectonic formations can be said to signify that the task of modelling this complexity normally succumbs either to idiosyncratic intuitionism or to overly rigid and simplistic categorization.[1]

In this chapter we will not attempt to classify all the possible ways in which architectonic formations signify. While the system of classification proposed here is largely unique, and to a certain extent cross-cuts a number of traditional ways of looking at the situation, it will not seek to model all of the facets of architectonic meaning. Instead, we shall offer a provisional classification whose purpose is to capture its most salient facets, which may serve as a template for future work.

In a general sense, every aspect of architectonic formation is meaningful in some sense. The various sign-types in the hierarchy of signs each carry their own kinds of meaningfulness: each functions in a particular way. Thus, the bundles of copresent distinctive features, and the sets of systemic units, are meaningful in different ways from directly-significative formations such as cells and matrices, as our analyses in the previous chapter have illustrated.

Architectonic significance is markedly different from linguistic meaning in part because of striking differences induced in each code by the nature of its signing medium and that medium's relative permanence. With regard to the first aspect, there is, as we have noted before, a marked difference between the two codes: the medium of the linguistic system is relatively homogeneous and narrowly circumscribed compared to the architectonic medium—which is potentially coterminous with the range of the material resources of the biosphere, including our own and other human bodies.

Various aspects of the linguistic signalling medium provide information, in a given speech act, about the identity of the speaker semi-independently of the context of the message itself. Perceptually, we are accustomed to recognize a given speaker by his voice-quality, idiosyncrasies of syntax, characteristic vocabulary, and so forth.

But there is a sense in which the architectonic correlate of the directly significative or sense-determinative aspect of acoustic signals is characteristically richer than its linguistic counterpart. This richness is a concomitant of the many aspects of architectonic materialization, including coloration, texture, material size, the modular patterning of materials, etc. In the built environment, the material organization of architectonic formations comprises a multidimensional system in its own right, which may be as fully complex as the formal system itself.

It is necessary to distinguish the *formal structure*[a] of an architectonic code from its *material structure*[a]. While materialization serves a systemic function in the realization of formal structure, it is also a semi-autonomous system in its own right, with its own domains of meaningfulness as specified by particular corpora.

A good example of the latter is the symbolic use of certain materials in a built environment, as noted by M. Wallis:[2]

> As testified by Berossos, author of the Greek-language work *Babyloniaka,* who lived under the successors of Alexander the great, every storey of the (ziggurat) was painted in the color of the corresponding heavenly body: the lowest was painted black (Saturn), the next ones were painted white (Venus), purple (Jupiter), blue (Mercury), red (Mars), silver (the Moon), and finally gold (the Sun).
>
> In the temples and palaces of Imperial Rome the dome was a *coeli imago.* In Nero's palace, called Domus Aurea, the round main hall had a dome that symbolized heaven and rotated day and night around its axis (Suetonius, *The Life of Nero*, Chap. XXXI).[3]

In the first example, the significative use of coloration is semi-autonomous of the actual materials used in construction of the ziggurat, and òf the geometric properties of the formal structure,[4] as well as of the actual metric sizes of the components. In the second example, what is principally significative is the formal structure in question (irrespective of the materials, actual size, coloration and texture, etc.).

In the latter case, the dome may have been painted blue with stars on it (painted gold), or black, or may have been painted half-black and half light-blue, and any manner of astrological figures may have been painted within the dome, to signify stellar constellations.

Architectural history is replete with countless examples of this kind of referential symbolism, and the variations among such possible situations is enormous. What is important for our purposes here is the evident *semi-autonomy* of the domains of signification alluded to—that of formal structure and that of materialization.

But the situation is more complex than that pictured here, for even though we are evidently dealing with the meaningfulness of two major components of architectonic formation, a more salient distinction in terms of meaningfulness *cuts across* both formal structure and material organization.

In the first example above, the geometric configuration of the ziggurat—its formal structure of masses and volumes—is directly significant with respect to a totality of religious and ritual associations. The meaningfulness of the ziggurat is an aggregate of both formal and material factors—i.e., both the geometric formation itself (semi-autonomously of size, materials used in construction, the texturing of materials, and so forth) as well as its physical realization with respect to specific and conventional materials, colors, sizes relative to other formations, etc.).

The significance of an architectonic formation is a *composite* of a variety of formative features drawn from various levels of systemic organization. A given formative feature may have a dual or multiple signification, depending upon our perspective on the totality of the formation. Thus the ceiling of a structure is simultaneously meaningful *systemically*, as a component in the formal definition of a space-cell, and may also be significant in a given corpus *sematectonically*, as in the case where the ceiling of a house or temple is intended to symbolize the heavens (in contrast to the walls, which may symbolize the four cardinal directions of the horizon, and in contrast to the floor—paved or not—which may symbolize the earth, the underworld, and so forth).

But sematectonic significance cross-cuts *both* formal and material structure, for not only may a ceiling be directly-significant with respect to its geometric configuration and position relative to other *forms*, the materiality of that *form*'s realization may also be directly or sematectonically significant—through the use of special materials, colors, textures, sizes, etc.

Meaningfulness, in other words, is a property of an architectonic code at *all* levels of its organization, and in a very real sense almost anything perceptually-palpable may be employed significantly, from subtle variations in color, texture and lighting to the geometric configurations of a formation, including not only the shapes of objects themselves (relative to other shapes), but also their relative placements. In the latter case, we may recall the organization of the Minoan hall system as comprising both certain kinds of space-cells *as well as* their relative arrangements as syntactic matrices. In our analysis of the hall system we saw that the same cellular formations occurring separately and non-contiguously have different meanings and functions. Moreover, the hall system as a whole was characteristically situated relative to other cell-aggregates in a house.[5]

It need not be stressed that the domains of significance are chiefly conventional and corpus-specific, so that given aspects of formal and material organization will be differently meaningful in different corpora or systems. It remains unclear to what extent we are justified at this stage in the development of architectonic analysis to speak confidently of universal domains of significa-tion, even though such domains may be claimed to exist.[6]

In the present chapter we will examine the question of architectonic meaning through a consideration of formal and material organization as well as systemic and sematectonic significance. But the problem of material organization will itself be discussed in more detail in the next chapter. Our chief concern in what follows here will be with the question of architectonic significance with respect to formal organization, and in particular the question of architectonic *function*[a], a subject which has had a long history of misunderstanding in the received literature. As we shall see, the semiotic nature of the built environment is saliently through a consideration of the *multi-functional* nature of the architectonic formation. This property of the architectonic system illuminates a number of important correlative features with other human sign-systems.

In addressing the question of architectonic meaning, any analysis will be most productive when the essential and fundamental difference between *meaning* and *reference* is clearly borne in mind. *Meaning* is the specification of an ordered trace of relationships which a given sign bears to other signs within the same code, whereas *reference* is not an indexical relationship which a given sign bears to formations outside of semiotic systems, toward some fictive 'real' world, but rather involves cross-modal associative implications. In verbal language, for example, 'shifters' are cross-modally indexical with respect to significative formations in a somatotopic modality (i.e., the relative placements and perspectival positionings of addressers and addressees in communicative events). In an identical fashion, the 'meaning' of a given architectonic construct is internal to its own code whereas its 'reference' may implicate a culturally-copresent set of texts, doctrines or beliefs, which themselves comprise significative formations in their own right in adjacent codes. And the relationships among all these may be metonymic or indexical, as well as metaphoric (i.e., indexical and 'iconic'). (For a further discussion of this problem, see the Appendix below.)

ARCHITECTONIC MULTIFUNCTIONALITY

A picture of the organization of architectonic functionality is often misconstrued with a classification of architectonic *types* (e.g., residential, industrial, religious, governmental, educational, and so forth). To be sure, at a given place and time, a corpus will manifest a characteristic typology of formations, each of which is conventionally (and to some extent temporarily) associated with certain usages. Not only are given usages defined differently from culture to culture, so also are the ranges of formal types. There can be no universal 'house' type because the notion of dwelling is a specific function of the definitions of a given society.[7] It is only the systemic sum of all architectonic types at a given place and time which characterizes the typological associations of individual formations.

In other words, the association between a formation and its referents in a given architectonic system is a *conventional* one. 'Homonymous' formations in two corpora only accidentally (if at all) suggest associations with exactly equivalent semantic domains. Both the identity and meaningfulness of architectonic formations are systemically-defined with relation to an ordered network of conventional associations, and conventional formations. These two domains or networks, moreover, behave semi-autonomously over time, each displaying a half-life of its own. Even though in formation they may bear a striking resemblance to each other, a basilica in 100 B.C. and one in 100 A.D. carry sharply differing associations with respect to usage (civic meeting hall *vs.* Christian church).

Formational typology provides us with a picture of the usages to which formations are put (i.e., with which they are associable) at a given time in a specific corpus—in other words, the ranges of their *referential* associations, their immediate 'purposes' or their contextual 'utility.' It need not, in addition, be stressed that 'form' does not 'follow' 'function' (in the sense of usage) any more than 'function follows form,' except in a temporary, provisional, conventional, and corpus-specific sense, bearing in mind that 'follows' cannot mean 'is determined by,' in any absolute sense. Within any culture there are ranges of alternative realization to any given 'function', whether that be time-telling, dwelling, making garments, or preparing food.

Clearly, the functionality of architectonic systems is a very complex matter, made superficially more complicated by a long history of the issue of 'functionalism' expounded by art historians and others—a subject today more of peripheral sociological import rather than of strictly architectonic interest.

It will be evident that architectonic formations are inherently *multifunctional* in nature, and that referential association or intended (and effective) *usage* is but *one dimension* of architectonic function. An architectonic object may be said to function *referentially*[a] through an orientation upon the contextual associations or usages which a corpus prescribes.

But such a function necessarily *coexists* with other functions which suggest differing orientations upon various components of the processes of architectonic semiosis. For example, the *aesthetic*[a] function of a formation may be dominant—in other words, there may be manifest a self-conscious orientation upon the formation itself as a transmitted sign or message. As with the referential functions of an object, the aesthetic function is similarly corpus-specific with respect to the aesthetic conventions of a society at a given time: a certain modular homogeneity may be manifest, wherein the component formations of an architectonic object are proportionally graded with respect to each other according to a conventional canon of 'harmonic' numerical ratios.

Yet proportional harmonics (or chromatic or textural harmonics) is only one of a wide variety of means, and each corpus at a given time and place will reveal its own version(s) of what it considers appropriately aesthetic.

While the aesthetic function may manifest itself in components less charged with referential association (for example color), it is not necessarily the case that the function is associated with one or another formational *type*: no one formational type is inherently more prone to manifest a dominance of the aesthetic function, even if it is the case that for a given corpus at a given time and place, the aesthetic function may be dominant (as with cathedrals or private dwellings, etc.). There is, moreover, no clear boundary between structures with an aesthetic function predominant and those with which it may play a lesser role.

Another function manifest by architectonic formations is that of an orientation upon the *code itself* of which it is a realization. This is normally realized architectonically through historical reference, as when a formation consciously alludes to a set of stylistic characterizations of non-currently-dominant formations.

Historical allusion takes many forms in architectonic systems, from pedantic recreations of famous landmarks, such as a copy of a classical temple (which may, however, manifest for its referential context non-historical usages, such as a stock exchange, etc.) to formations whose outer facade only simulates an historical prototype (as where a multistoreyed trolley-barn has a facade articulated like a Renaissance palazzo or an Ostian apartment house). The allusion, moreover, may also be cross-systemic, as where a restaurant in a contemporary western city is articulated to represent a Polynesian hut.

Such a function, which we may term *meta-architectonic*[a], since in the broadest sense it calls into conscious attention an architectonic code itself, coexists with the aforementioned functions to a greater or lesser degree of dominance. A formation may function meta-architectonically to a very minimal degree, wherein allusory reference is confined to details of material articulation such as baseboard moldings, or maximally, as in the case where a house in Wisconsin purports to be a Spanish hacienda. Allusory reference may also be quite subtle, as where the proportions of a contemporary villa simulate the modular proportional scheme of famous historical prototypes (e.g., certain Renaissance palazzi—which themselves may simulate the modular organization of a Roman building simulating a Greek temple, etc.): the discussions by Colin Rowe in his *Mathematics of the Ideal Villa and Other Essays* (1976) are especially illustrative in this regard. The picture of architectonic function is clearly broader than the range of referential uses alone, and it would appear to be the case that architectonic formations may manifest a variety of dimensions or orientations upon the various aspects of architectonic semiosis itself.

In addition to its referential, aesthetic and allusory functions, architectonic objects also function *territorially*[a] by staging behavioral routines or episodes, framing interpersonal interactions, and dividing, structuring, delimiting, or zoning an environment. While it establishes a referential context of usages, for example, the organization of a neighborhood may be such as to define a common focus (around a small plaza, or on both sides of a certain portion of a boulevard), a common ground for groups of people with certain social, ethnic, economic or religious ties. To an outsider, the neighborhood or quarter may be read merely as a transition from one part of a city to another, but for the insider these same formations articulate a social topology.

The territorial or 'phatic'[a] function is realized in many different ways in different corpora, and moreover changes over time and place within a large corpus. In some cases, the presence of an object may be predominantly phatic or territorial—as with a wall or a grown hedge, even a church in a neighborhood.[8] But these same objects reveal coexistent aesthetic, referential and allusory dimensions: the particular hierarchy of dominance or strength of one dimension over another or others may vary from one formation in a corpus to another.

Mukařovský correctly saw architecture as an example *par excellence* of a multifunctional system, differing from other instrumentalities of human activity as complex as machines by being conventionally connected to any kind of activity and designed to serve as a spatial milieu for the most varied behavior:

> Architecture organizes the space surrounding man. It organizes this space as a whole and with respect to man in his entirety, that is with respect to all the physical or psychic actions of which man is capable and of which a building can become the setting. When we say that architecture organizes this space as a whole, we mean that none of the parts of architecture has functional independence but that each of them is evaluated only according to how it forms—motorically or optically—the space into which it is incorporated and which it delimits.[9]

Architecture, he says, organizes space with respect to man in his entirety, that is, with respect to all the physical or mental activities of which he is capable.

He goes on to delimit what he terms five *functional horizons* of architecture.[10] A building's function is determined by (1) an immediate purpose (corresponding broadly to our referential usage-context); by (2) an historical purpose, wherein functionality is "governed not only by an immediate practical consideration but also by a fixed canon (or set of norms) for this kind of structure and its previous development."[11] This corresponds to the meta-architectonic or allusory and code-oriented functional dimensions.

A building manifests a functional horizon created, thirdly, by "the organization of the collective to which the client and architect belong,"[12] corresponding generally to the phatic-territorial function discussed above, "in accordance with the organization of society, the available economic and material possibilities, and so forth."

A fourth functional horizon is the aesthetic, wherein, when this is in dominance, it "renders the thing itself as the purpose."[13] He would concur with our view that there is not an object-*type* which necessarily has to be its vehicle, rightly seeing the aesthetic function as *one* of the semiotic *functions*.

But it is in the area of his fifth architectonic function, what he terms the individual functional horizon, where his picture of functionality becomes, from our point of view, somewhat ambiguous. He states, correctly, that "an individual can obviously deviate from everything which has been set as a norm by the preceding horizons."[14] He sees this as a *violation* of functionality deriving from the decision of an individual, whether client or architect.

There exist, however, a number of significant differences between the two types of "violation." The situation may be clarified by considering the nature of designer-builder-architect and the person(s) 'addressed' by the processes of architectonic semiosis or transmission *vis-à-vis* apparently similar components in verbal semiosis.

In speaking of architectonic function, we have been considering sets of contrastive associations among, and orientations upon, the various components of a transmission. The process of architectonic transmission comprises several different components which recall—but are evidently not exactly coterminous with—the components of a verbal message.

In the case of the latter, the components include a speaker, the transmitter of a message, and a listener or receiver of the message, in addition to the transmission itself as a formation. In a linguistic system, the speaker himself will produce the formation with the instrumentality of his own speech organs. In an architectonic system, there may be a personal distinction between what are traditionally referred to as a designer and a builder (or builders). In other words, the initiator of an architectonic transmission may not in fact 'construct' that transmission, but may instead present to others for realization a simulative model or diagram of the intended transmission. Those 'others' may include the 'client' himself.

On the other side, the intended receiver of the transmission may be the transmitter himself (as may be the case in verbal language) or one or more others. Once 'transmitted', an architectonic formation continues to broadcast widely. Moreover, the personal identity of the receivers is not necessarily constant, and generations of individuals may continue to 'receive' an archaic transmission, as we have suggested above in connection with the question of relative permanence of signalling.

Furthermore, the various referential associations of a given formation may change over time, whether or not the receiver(s) of a transmission materially alter the construct, so that it is often the case that architectonic formations become increasingly polysemous[a], or semantically denser, over time. Even ruins have a romance.

In this regard, seen from the perspective of a settlement itself, a corpus will reveal layered strata of associations of greater or lesser depth. Formations in a built environment manifest different relative ages, histories of evolution, and ranges of association, much like lexico-grammatical components of a linguistic system. Of course the diachrony isn't necessarily in the direction of polysemous density; categories also merge, simplify and coalesce over time. Certain distinctions may become mute or irrelevant.

This situation is in large part an artifact of the relative permanence of some architectonic signs, which remain in the reified memory store of a society to interact with and influence later formations. This is somewhat analogous to a situation in linguistic systems wherein sets of recorded speech acts will interact with the daily speech of later generations, although strictly speaking the analogy also overlaps with another situation manifest in architectonic evolution in certain corpora wherein records of earlier *designs* (old plans, models, even verbal texts of specifications) may influence current practice.[15]

Another corollary of this situation is that architectonic evolution is in no way linear or logical *in se*, but is (as with any semiotic system in its diachrony) a function of the complexly-integrated evolution of a culture itself, in its totality.[16]

Hence the nature of the architectonic system induces code-specific types of relationships between what in a linguistic frame might be called 'addresser' and 'addressee'. In the former code, the 'speaker-hearer' of linguistics exists, as a relationship in normal semiosis, as but one of a complex set of possible relationships. But such complexities also exist in verbal semiosis, although they are not as characteristically well delineated as the simpler, idealized transmission state.[17]

In the architectonic code, the original 'generator' of a formation may be a person or persons who 'design' a formation who may also (but need not) 'construct' that formation for a 'client' (who may be the generator or builder) who employs the formation significantly (and thus in a sense serves as a 'transmitter' of that signal to himself (or themselves) or to others—or both). In an idealized sense, and in a manner homologous to 'speaker-hearer' transmission in verbal language, there exists an 'addresser', an 'addressee', and a (more or less permanent) 'message' or transmission. But there are patently a wide variety of possible realizations of the various components of the transmission, of semiosis.

These differences from the processes of linguistic semiosis are a corollary of the nature of the signing medium itself, the relative object-permanence of the sign-formation, and the nature of the variant usages or contextual referents of that semiosis. Nevertheless, the fundamental semioses of both systems are clearly homologous.

Consequently, the 'functional deviation' on the part of 'addressees' cannot strictly speaking be considered a function in and of the code itself except insofar as there are corpus-specific constraints upon meaning, usage or interpretation. Such 'violation' is allowable to varying degrees by different systems principally as an artifact of the *conventionality* of built environments as systems of signs. Conventionality is a property of codes, and not a function.

'Functional deviation' on the part of the 'addresser', however, does in fact relate to one of the functions of architectonic transmissions, insofar as it refers to an orientation upon the signer(s) or makers themselves. In this sense, an architectonic formation may reveal an emphasis upon various aspects of the identity or identities of 'addresser(s)'—as in the case where a formation manifests sense-determinative cues as to the orientation of the addresser(s) upon the various components of architectonic semiosis.

A formation may bear the mark of a 'personal style' through palpable deviations or idiosyncratic realizations of (for example) sets of corpus-specific historical norms, or of common referential associations, aesthetic norms, or phatic-territorial norms.

Such an *orientation* recalls the 'emotive'[a] functions of a linguistic message, wherein a speaker will give cues as to his particular orientation upon a given subject. Thus, the statement 'New York is very far from here' reveals the particular emotive perspective of a speaker by contrast with a statement oriented upon the referential context, such as 'New York is ten miles from here'.

In a linguistic code, the 'emotive' orientation may be cued by a very wide variety of means—intonation, stress, the use of certain lexical items, etc.

In a similar fashion, a built environment patently reveals an emotive or *expressive*[a] orientation upon the identity of an 'addresser' through corpus-specific means. An outsider or child may have to learn a large number of subtle cues as to whether a given construct manifests a personal, expressive, stylistic deviance from a conventional set of norms. Moreover, such cues may be realized both in details of geometric or spatial formation and in the use of certain kinds of materials, colors, textures, and so forth. In addition, cues may be found with respect to the associative usages prescribed by a formation's components. If kitchens are conventionally square in plan while bedrooms are conventionally 1:2 rectangles in plan, a formation which idiosyncratically reverses these contextual associations will be expressive of the particular perspective on these norms on the part of the addresser.

It is important in this regard to understand that the 'addresser' in such a case may be *either* the original generator of the design of the construct (or his surrogates), *or* the 'user' of that formation—as in the case where a 'client' expressively reorganizes a house in a way which deviates from the norms set out unambiguously by the 'generator'. *In this instance, the 'user' functions as a signer or addresser vis-à-vis* himself and others. Once again, the ability to do this is itself a concomitant property of the architectonic code in contrast to some others, wherein the 'roles' of addresser and addressee are not necessarily coterminous with a simple 'speaker-hearer' relationship, and which moreover is an artifact of the particular 'medium' or channel of the code, whose constraints are different from those of nonvisual codes.

Architectonic multifunctionality is manifest, then, as sets of relative orientations upon the various components of the processes of semiosis. In addition, a given function will achieve greater or lesser dominance in a given transmission with respect to coeval functions. Furthermore, since architectonic transmissions remain perceptually available, they are open to highly complex and subtle reorientations over time, so that a function which may be dominant over others at the time of a formation's generation may be replaced in favor of other orientations or functions, either immediately or over many generations. It is more than simply a matter of static, idiosyncratic reinterpretation: it is in fact a reorganization and re-transmission of a sign which continues to 'broadcast' in subtle and ironic dynamic synchrony. The *addresser* of an architectonic transmission is the person or persons who use an architectonic formation.

FUNCTIONAL CORRELATIVITY[a]

Thus, while we would concur generally with Mukařovský's picture of architectural polyfunctionality, it is clear that his model is ambiguous with regard to the maker-client relationship in the processes of semiosis.

Thus far, our explication of architectonic multifunctionality suggests the following picture. In architectonic semiosis, an orientation

(1)	upon 'usage' or semantic context	=	the referential function;
(2)	upon the formation itself	=	the aesthetic function;
(3)	upon the code or system	=	the meta-architectonic or allusory function;
(4)	upon the maintenance of contact	=	the phatic-territorial function;
(5)	upon the 'addresser' (q.v.)	=	the expressive or emotive function.

The resultant picture clearly resonates with the conception of linguistic multifunctionality devised by Jakobson and others[18] wherein the orientations upon various components of a transmission delineate a variety of functions, each of which may be in greater or lesser dominance with respect to others which may be co-occurrent in the same transmission.

According to Jakobson's formulation, an orientation upon:

(1)	the context	=	the semantico-referential function;[19]
(2)	the message itself	=	the poetic function;
(3)	the code itself	=	the metalinguistic function;
(4)	maintenance of contact between speaker and hearer	=	the phatic function;
(5)	the addresser	=	the emotive function;

and, in addition, an orientation upon

(6) the addressee   = the conative or exhortative function.

It may be asked if the architectonic system reveals a functional orientation correlative to the conative-exhortatory function in verbal language. The answer is patent, once we are clear about the coexistent nature of functions in architectonic formations. Environmental objects do in fact carry exhortations to channel, constrain and routinize spatiokinetic behavior by the very fact that they serve to *stage* behaviors (*sc.*, they indicate certain ranges of referential association).

This function is manifest in a very wide variety of ways in different corpora. This is not to say that architectonic and linguistic conation are coterminous with respect to behavioral activity. Certain equivalencies are patent, of course, but not all. I can guard my privacy either by shouting at persons who approach to 'keep out!', or I can build a wall, with a gate to which only I have a key.

I can also signal my intentions redundantly by building a high wall and posting a written message reading 'keep out'; indeed multimodal conation and its concomitant perceptual augmentation would appear to be the norm in human societies.

By virtue of the fact that any verbal message stands to influence the behavior of a listener, the conative function may normally be present in verbal semiosis. In a similar fashion, by virtue of the fact that an architectonic formation—a built environment—necessarily channels behavior in a wide variety of ways, the phatic-territorial function of architectonic semiosis is essentially coexistent with its conative orientation. But clearly the two are not coterminous, any more than the phatic and conative functions of verbal semiosis are. In part, the distinction lies in the *vector of emphasis,* and the orientation upon different semiotic components of a transmission.

Linguistic conation comprises exhortation which is only in part territorial or addressed *to* spatiokinesis; architectonic conation addresses 'addressees' *through* a spatiokinetic medium in order to achieve a variety of conceptual ends.

A given building may place heavy emphasis upon (what a generator or a society may regard as) efficient 'circulation'. In this case, a formation will provide users with a variety of motor-optical cues which carry information as to how to get from point A to point B within a building, or how to reach an exit in case of fire or divine wrath, or how to behave in a polite fashion when going through a doorway.

These ends may be achieved in a great many corpus-specific ways—from the shaping of corridors to a heavy articulation of components of a formation such as doorways which prescribe certain routines of formal entrance, to conventionally-understood color-codings of elements, to verbal signs and arrows, to red-amber-and-green traffic signals.[20]

The ball of red thread unravelled by Ariadne for the use of Theseus in escaping the lair of the minotaur at the center of the Knossian labyrinth is a clear example of architectonic conation (in this case tantalizingly supported by a particular archaeological find).[21]

The addressee may be exhorted to 'follow the yellow brick road' to reach a certain goal, and the Spanish Steps may have called forth certain spatiokinetic rhythms in the behavior of their initial addressees.

It need not be stressed that conative emphases differ from one corpus to another; whatever may be trans-societal in perceptual address, human perceptual mechanisms are socialized into conventional norms: a doorway twice human scale may be either uplifting or intimidating, forbidding or inviting, even in the same breath. Nor do red brick sidewalks necessarily lead to minotaurs.[22]

The picture of multifunctionality observable in built environments patently calls forth linguistic correspondences which are more *correlative*[a] than coterminous, as we have suggested above:

architectonic semiosis				linguistic semiosis		
orientation		function		orientation		function
context	:	referential	::	context	:	referential
formation	:	aesthetic	::	message	:	poetic
code	:	allusory	::	code	:	metalinguistic
contact	:	territorial	::	contact	:	phatic
addresser	:	expressive	::	speaker	:	emotive
addressee	:	exhortative	::	hearer	:	conative

It should be borne in mind that such correlations comprise broad equivalencies, given the patent differences in the two sign systems. The two systems are not isofunctional in any given culture, and their redundancies overlap in a dynamic manner. They are not two ways of 'doing the same thing', they are partly-redundant modalities in multimodal social communication, designed to reinforce each other in some respects, while simultaneously offering different advantages, under contrastive circumstances.

The built environment may provide a matrix or template for behavior, but it is not a static template, it is continually palimpsested as a result of that behavior, and is never the same at two points in time, even if to the unaware it might 'look' the same. The same patently applies to verbal language.

It cannot be maintained that 'architecture' is merely four-dimensional language any more than it can be claimed that architecture is simply frozen music; nor can it be claimed that language is merely architecture in Flatland. Whatever architectonic and linguistic systems share, they share features by virtue of their generic functions as human semiotic systems. As such, they patently reveal correlative processes of formation and signification.

Nor can it be maintained that the one is a blank ground to the other's figure, however momentarily useful it might be to so represent them in analysis, and even when they so appear to operate with respect to each other for specific purposes.[23] They each provide a partially-overlapping perspective on the totalities of a society's culture, on its particular world, much like two sets of sensory organs which together and in close concert respond to different features of a percept to build an overall composite reality.

We cannot adequately understand the structure and operant functions of either modality without an understanding of its cross-indexed complement/supplement. There are too many loose threads in each modality when analyzed with one eye. Moreover, our view of each will also be a function of our perspective on the organization of culture itself as a multi-modal system of sign systems.[24]

In addition, in attempting to understand the nature of architectonic functionality it will be important to have some understanding of the origins of the system in human evolution. Although this subject is outside of the realm of interests of the present volume,[25] the generic subject of the purposes of the built environment vis-à-vis other sign-systems lies at the heart of our present concerns, and we have attempted to address this issue through various perspectives.

At the beginning of this section, we discussed briefly the problem of the material organization of architectonic formations, and it is to this question that we shall presently turn.

Before addressing these questions, we need to say a word about the nature of what we have generically termed in this chapter the 'association' of a formation and its 'referent meanings'. If it is in fact the case that architectonic formations are multifunctional in orientation, revealing a variety of coexistent orientations upon the several components of architectonic semiosis, then how may we characterize the geometries of that associability? What kind or kinds of relationships exist between a given formation and its associated referents?

The architectonic *sign* comprises a formation (*signans*)[a] or that-which-signifies, plus its referent (*signatum*)[a], or that-which-is-signified. In concurring generally with the Peircean notion of 'meaning' as a translation or transmutation connecting one medium (e.g., a material formation) with another (e.g., a set of behaviors or a set of cognitive domains—which may include the formation itself),[26] we can assert that such translational connectivities are of several types.

The relationship between a formation and its referent may, for example, be of an *iconic*[a] nature, wherein the formation purports to resemble its referent in varying degrees. Thus, a construct which purports to simulate or model, in the syntactic association of its component parts, a certain conceptual order (e.g., a society's image of its cosmos), may function as an iconic sign. The great stupa-mountain of Borobudur in Java may thus be seen as an iconic sign in that its parts are assembled to portray an idealized cosmic structure.

Iconism in the architectonic code may be manifested along a scale of resemblance from the patently pictorial or figurative to the generically diagrammatic. In the case of Borobudur, the construct is in fact a model of the Buddhist universe, organized to be perceived spatiotemporally as a life-passage from the chaotic depths of mortal despair to the heights of heavenly harmony and oneness. A simple example of a more diagrammatic iconicity would be the organization of the component parts of a construct so that their relative proportions and placement embody, say, the idealized proportions of the human body.

Architectonic iconism may involve some aspect of conventional *symbolism*[a], wherein the component parts of a formation generically resemble the relative placement of body parts (or 'parts' of a body politic, such as the communion of the faithful), while depending for their iconicity upon cultural and conventional associations, as in the case where the parts of a christian church purport an association with parts of the 'body' of the church as an institution—the bricks being said to be the aggregate of the individual faithful, the mortar joining them christian love or charity, etc.[27]

In a general sense, architectonic constructs serve as iconic signs in that their spatiotemporal organization obversely simulates or models the behavioral geometry of episodic routines. It may be questioned if iconism in the architectonic code is ever really 'pure' rather than being characteristically admixed with aspects of conventional and corpus-specific symbolism. Nor for that matter is a snapshot a 'pure' icon.[28]

A symbolic sign would be one in which the relationship between *signans* and *signatum* is the result of conventional association. Icons and symbols are characteristically admixed such that most iconic signs will be at least partly symbolic, and vice-versa.[29]

Architectonic and linguistic signs evidently differ with respect to the characteristic dominance of different kinds of *signans-signatum* relationships. Iconism may be more prevalent in architectonic systems than in languages, but it is clear that both codes are primarily symbolic in nature, and their varying degrees of iconicity may be merely an artifact of more fundamental differences between the systems with respect to medium, permanence and dimensionality.

In a Peircean frame, architectonic signs may also be of an *indexical*[a] nature, wherein certain formations bear a relationship of immediate contiguity to their referents. The familiar examples of a traffic signal or visual arrow come to mind, but in such a perspective we would also have to admit doors and walls as functioning indexically with respect to their contiguous association with operant behaviors such as entering and exiting vis-à-vis other loci.

But even such indexical signs as the red-amber-green traffic signal are coevally symbolic or conventional, since it has not been demonstrated that their particular contrastive colors will inherently trigger invariant reactions among all humans, except insofar as a society has made an arbitrary association between 'red' and 'stopping' in contrast to 'green' and 'proceeding'.

In addition to the evident fact that in an architectonic system signs will be inherently admixed with respect to symbolism, iconity and indexicality, it is also pertinent to note that architectonic and linguistic codes do not inherently contrast with respect to purported differences in the 'gradiency' or non-binary contrastiveness of sign formation. As is now patent, architectonic signification parallels that of verbal language in relying upon perceptually-palpable distinctions and disjunctions in formation, whose contrastive oppositions in formation purport to signal differences in conceptual information and association. Both systems employ binary contrastive oppositions *as well as* complex relative gradiences. Despite claims in both directions, the particular 'mix' of the two may not be all that different: the more we understand of the nature and organization of architectonic (and in general visual) semiosis, the more it becomes apparent that the purported 'gradiency' of architectonic signals is a corollary of corpus-specific differences in medium, functions, usages, and the nature of the perceptual mechanisms addressed and employed.

Architectonic and linguistic systems signify in processually-equivalent ways; they do not present an absolute black and white contrast to each other, and they are designed to operate in the context of each other. Their semantic domains dynamically overlap and implicate each other.

Where one offers a palpable categorization in a broad range, the other may specify detailed significative distinctions. Whether there exists a lexical item for a Hopi 'kiva' or not,[30] the architectonic system incorporates a certain distinctive configuration (and vice-versa). Where one system may point with a narrow finger, the other may broadly gesture. But each system does both, in culture-specific, code-specific, and conventionally symbolic ways.

Both systems present a people with complementary and supplementary perspectives on a sociocultural world, and both are intended to serve as 'common codes' for different reasons and at different times, as well as in partly-redundant and dynamic synchronization.

The received classification of signs as indexical, iconic and symbolic may or may not turn out to be useful in the long run. We simply need to know much more about the nature and organization of nonlinguistic semiosis. This in turn will affect our picture of linguistic signs.[31]

I suspect that a further explication of the phenomena of *metaphor* and *metonymy* will shed light on this problem, for it is evident that the Peirceian "iconic" and "indexical" relations are subsumed under these categories, with the notion of "symbol" reserved for generic conventional semiotic signing of any type (see below, Appendix).

Furthermore, we should be wary of using such categories as necessary indicators of stages in conceptual ontogenesis (as, for example, where a symbolic sign is taken as inherently more conceptually advanced than, say, an iconic sign, or an indexical sign). It remains unclear to what extent one sign-type necessarily implies the prior existence of one or both of the other.

This unclarity is in part the result of ambiguities in the fossil record. It has not been entirely clear *what kind* of ontogenetic formal evidence is really needed to support a picture of linear, componential evolution of sign-types.[32]

FOOTNOTES

CHAPTER IV

[1]A good sample of the kinds of approaches to architectonic meaning may be found in C. Jencks, ed., *Meaning in Architecture*, New York, 1970.

[2]M. Wallis, "Semantic and Symbolic Elements in Architecture: Iconology as a First Step Towards an Architectural Semiotic," in M. Wallis, *Arts & Signs* (Studies in Semiotics 2), Bloomington, Indiana, 1975, pp. 50-51.

[3]*Ibid*., with extensive references, p. 51.

[4]Semi-autonomous, that is, in the sense of being non-necessary. A given color is not necessarily tied to a given geometric shape but may be copresent with other shapes (and vice-versa). See also our discussion above in Chapter II.

[5] See above, Chapter II, section on "Formative Units."

[6]See our discussion below in Chapter V.

[7] See Preziosi, *Origins* . . . , Chapter III.

[8]Or a 'local city hall', or community center, etc.

[9]J. Mukařovský, *op. cit*., 240.

[10]*Ibid*., 241 ff.

[11]*Ibid*., 242.

[12]*Id*.; the author further suggests that various nuances of the symbolic function are also incorporated into this functional horizon.

[13]*Ibid*., 244.

[14]*Ibid*., 242.

[15] The most familiar example being the period of the European Renaissance, wherein ancient paradigms and models were rediscovered, or reinvented; similarly during the Neoclassical period during which classical archaeology arose in part as a handmaiden of architectural practice (applied architectonics).

[16]For a lucid discussion of the problem, see G. Kubler, *The Shape of Time*, New Haven, 1965.

[17] See M. Silverstein, *op. cit*., 21 ff.

[18]R. Jakobson, "Linguistics and Poetics," in T. Sebeok, ed., *Style in Language*, Bloomington, Indiana, 1960, 350-377.

[19]M. Silverstein, *loc. cit.* gives an interesting account of the place of 'semantic' meaningfulness in speech arts.

[20]That is to say, each architectonic system will incorporate a variety of parastructural formations in transmission of information, often providing a large amount of redundancy or perceptual enhancement over and above the 'syntactic' aggregation of formations.

[21]I.e., a thin red border along the lower part of the walls of the main corridor linking the central court of the Knossian palace with the western outer entrance.

[22]See in this regard the work of K. Lynch cited in the Bibliography.

[23]See Preziosi, 1978k.

[24]For a discussion of the 'design features' of cultures, see Preziosi, *Origins* . . . , Chapter V, section 2, and see the Appendix below.

[25] Discussed in Preziosi, *Origins* . . . , Chapter II.

[26]That is to say, the aesthetic function, wherein *signans* = *signatum*. This contrasts with the notions elaborated by R. Barthes, *Mythologies*, Paris, 1957, esp. p. 115; see the commentary by T. Hawkes on the subject in his *Semiotics and Structuralism*, Berkeley, 1977, Chapter 3.

[27] See M. Wallis, *op. cit*., 39-58.

[28]With respect to photographic images, we may discern a correlative multifunctionality grounded in differential reference-orientations: Photography vs. snapshots recalling the dominance of an aesthetic orientation vs. other kinds of orientation (phatic, conative, etc.).

[29]See U. Eco's important critique of the Peirceian trichotomies in U. Eco, *A Theory of Semiotics*, Bloomington, Indiana, 1976, 191 ff.

[30]B. L. Whorf, *Language, Thought & Reality*, Cambridge, Mass., 1956, 199 ff.

[31]See U. Eco, *loc. cit.*

[32]See Preziosi, *Origins* . . . , Chapter IV.

Chapter V
Material Organization

INTRODUCTION

In our introductory chapter, we noted that equivalent geometric forms may exhibit variation in a large number of ways with respect to *materialization*. In other words, two space-cells X_1 and X_2 of identical geometric configuration—for example cubic—may contrast with respect to (1) metric *size* (wherein X_1 is 5 x 5 meters, and X_2 is 6 x 6 x 6 meters), (2) *medium* (wherein X_1 is made up of timber and X_2 is made up of mud-brick + timber), (3) *texture* (wherein X_1 is made up of timber which has been left rough-hewn or unfinished and X_2 is made up of timber which has been smoothly sanded and finished), (4) *color* (wherein X_1 is unpainted (grey) cinder block and X_2 is painted white).

It will be evident that two given cubic cells may contrast on all of these axes, or several, or only one, or none. In addition, two cubic cells may be identical in all respects except that their relative positions in an aggregate or cluster of cells results in the former being sunny and well-lit and the latter dark and dank. Furthermore, two identical cells may contrast with regard to their relative acoustic environments: the former may be situated in a cluster overlooking a busy street, while the latter, only two doors away, is snug and quiet at the same time of day. Various constructional materials have different acoustic (as well as thermal or insulating) properties, and a very great degree of variation in such properties may be observed, all dependent upon complex relationships of size, media, texture and color. Two cells identical in all material respects except color, for example, may as a result contrast with respect to relative warmth or coolness.

The implication here of course is that all these (often extremely subtle) differences in materialization may be associated with different meanings or usages, and the presence of certain material properties may be highly significant for individuals and societies. Often such associations provide a culture with a "vocabulary" of contrasts which, while seemingly irrelevant to an outsider, project conventionally important contrasts of meaning to the society itself. What is a random stick in the ground to an outsider may be the central *axis mundi* of a village. The history of human relations is saturated with misunderstandings arising from this paradoxical situation. And yet this paradox lies at the core of the organization of architectonic systems. It may well also be that properties of illusion, paradox, ambiguity and camouflage are built into the nature of architectonic systems, and may have contributed to the adaptive advantages such systems have over pre-human built environments.[1]

As just noted, subtle differences in materialization may be mapped onto highly contrastive meaningful associations; in addition, it is evident that corpora contrast in this regard so that in society *A*, rough-textured architectonic objects are conventionally associated with secular construction, while in society *B* the reverse is the case. Even in situations where objects are positionally related to a cosmology mapped onto the geometry of the human body (left *vs.* right, up *vs.* down, front *vs.* back), the significance of a given position or orientation will differ: "left" may be lucky or unlucky, and "north" may be "up" or "down," good or evil. Moreover, even within the same society (no matter how small its population), different classes or clans may reverse the connotative geometry constant for another class or group. And both may change over time.

The question of the "inherent" meanings of given colors or textures or media or sizes (relative to the human form) is a vexed one, and we do not yet fully or securely understand what may be cross-culturally constant, or why it may be so. We shall consider this issue in the next section; for the moment consider the question of color symbolism.

For much of the Palaeolithic and Neolithic periods in human history, a great many human skeletal remains are found with traces of applied red coloring. Moreover, this is not limited to any one geographical area of the world, but recurs on several continents among groups which apparently had no contact with each other. It might seem that we could generalize from this phenomenon and claim that for human beings the association "red = blood = death" is in some way innate. But we must be careful here; for while human blood is normally reddish in color, the phenomenon of death being associated with spilled blood does not always hold, and the associations of death with other aspects of a cognitive system may for some relate to other colorings —say something on the "cool" end of the spectrum, e.g., blue, since from this point of view, a dead body is cool while live ones are warm.

We can go on indefinitely. But the apparent fact remains that *whatever may be innate in color* (or material or texture or size) *symbolism, such associations are expressed through systems of meaning founded upon conventional relational mechanisms.* An object magnified from human size to twice that size may be uplifting or threatening or ambiguously both; and its conventional associations for a given group will be a function of its position in an overall architectonic system of contrasts as much as it is directly relatable to the absolute metric size of any adult human.

Our chief concern in this chapter is two-fold. First, we shall consider the relationship between formal configuration and structure and the physical or material variations exhibited by such entities and aggregates. Secondly, we will explore the organization of material organization itself both for our analytic corpus and for architectonic systems in general. Both of these questions, clearly, are interrelated.

MATERIAL ORGANIZATION AND FORMAL STRUCTURE

It has been noted that given formal configurations—for example geometrically identical space-cells—may exhibit variation with respect to metric size, media, color, texture, etc. Furthermore, among the four latter, cells may exhibit a variety of contrasts, or combinations of features. For example, a given entity /E/ (wall) may contrast with another wall otherwise identical on three out of these four axes:

	/E/$_1$	/E/$_2$
size:	¼ x 3 x 5 m.	¼ x 3 x 5 m.
medium:	mud brick	mud brick
texture:	smooth	smooth
color:	unpainted	*whitewashed*

In addition, material variation may be observed in other respects which modify the relative appearances of the two entities. For example, with respect to medium, the bricks might be laid horizontally in one case, or in a herringbone pattern in the other; or the wall may be two brick-thicknesses or three, thereby contrasting with respect to size as well. In the former case, we are dealing with what we may term *composition*[a], an aspect which relates to all three latter items (medium, texture, and color).

Hence a wall /E/$_n$ will exhibit a tridimensional compositional aspect incorporating (a) the arrangement of medium, texture and color relative to each other, and (b) an internal relationship of parts on each count. Thus, regarding the latter, a wall may be composed, with respect to medium, as a vertical layering of (1) a rubble-stone foundation course; (2) an "ashlar" or finely-squared row of limestone blocks; on top of which is (3) a dozen rows of mud-bricks; surmounted by a course of squared timber near the ceiling level; this will contrast, moreover with other walls otherwise identical with respect to size, texture and color:

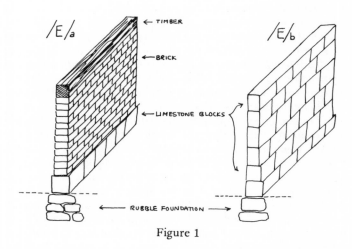

Figure 1

In the diagram, walls /E/$_a$ and /E/$_b$ contrast as indicated; consider both as painted ochre and smooth in texture, and of the same metric size. In addition, our /E/$_b$ may contrast with an /E/$_c$ made up of *gypsum* blocks but of the same composition, etc.

It becomes evident that such variations as may occur can multiply into the transfinite. How can we conceivably specify the range of all this material variety? This question becomes even more pressing when it is considered that architectonic systems appear to be realizable in material construction of nearly any conceivable type, drawing upon the physical resources of the planet in every ecological niche—from blocks of limestone to blocks of frozen water to the skins of animals to a shaded canopy provided by a cluster of trees in a forest.

Another complication arises: the resources of an ecological niche may be employed differently by different societies or different settlements in a niche belonging to the same society; in other words, *the "boundaries" of routines of material usage will not necessarily be coterminous with the temporal or geographical "boundaries" of a corpus.* Nor will it be necessarily found that contrastive corpora employ contrastive material syntactic modes. For example, the architectonic systems of Minoan Crete and Mycenaean Greece are clearly contrastive in terms of formal syntax, and yet we find, by and large, that the same materials are employed in expression, often in nearly identical ways, even across sub-routines of composition.

Whereas in sum, the two corpora contrast both formally and materially (and certainly functionally), many of the details of material expression are identical, although the use of materials *in relationship to* such aspects as size, texture, coloration and composition will be found to be different. Same ecological resources, different systemic usages.

Hence, it would be wisest to eschew an approach to our problem which smacks of "ecological determinism" wherein the material expression of a corpus is constrained to a narrow band of available resources.[2] In other words, those resources which a culture exploits will be only in part a direct function of what appears to be "objectively" available to an outsider (or insider). At the same time, what is seen is also a function of what a society of individuals *chooses to see* for reasons which may be only peripherally related to the "grammar" of an architectonic system *in se*. Constraints upon the choice of materials are inevitably found to be a result of cosmological, political, economic, technological, and other factors—factors which, along with architectonic and linguistic ones, comprise in large part the cognitive "map" a society has of itself. In other words, such constraints arise out of an equilibrated network of cognitive relationships, with each factor in some way a reflection of some or all of the others.

Moreover, the cognitive map of a culture is diachronically mutable, and subject to changes in its components over time in lesser or greater ways, and even differently or at different rates according to its components. Technological change may be more or less rapid than economic, and so forth.

But if we eschew an ecological determinism in the constraints upon the exploitation of ecological resources, we would at the same time need to recognize relative *limits* on such exploitation. It is clearly the case that such constraints will be broader than a deterministic view would suggest, and yet limited in some way. It may be well to bear in mind one of our observations above— namely that such constraints will be *simultaneously* ecological and cultural or systemic.

We might consider that constraints upon material expression represent a simultaneous projection of factors onto a common expressive plane. Some of these factors will be derived from the nature of the formal structure of a corpus itself; others will be 'external' to the architectonic system.[3]

In other words, it would appear that what we have come to call "material structure" is partly architectonic in origin, and partly "cultural" or "external" to an architectonic system *per se*. And even though material structure is bound up with a seemingly finite range of physical choice, that range is inevitably bound up with how it is "seen" or processed by a society. That is to say, material structure is *simultaneously* bound up with architectonic and extra-architectonic factors. It might be useful to consider, then, that material syntax or composition functions in the overall architectonic system as an "interface" between a "core" set of formal orderings and the external, physical world.

If we broaden our perspective, it would then appear that metaphorically the architectonic system in some way *mediates* between what we may term the *cognitive environment* and the *physical environment*. It is important to note here that by material structure or composition is *not* meant the actual physically-realized objects of a corpus, but rather the *geometry or logic of representation* specific to a corpus of forms. In other words, material structure will be seen as a complexly-ordered series of mappings which mediate between a core set of formal or geometric orderings and the physical environment itself.

To reiterate: the architectonic system *in toto* mediates between a "cognitive environment" and the "physical environment," whereas material structure mediates between an innermost or core formal structure and the physical environment.

But what does "material structure" itself comprise? Does it manifest an internal "structure" of its own which tends to be invariant across corpora?

We have noted a number of *aspects* of material structure above: size, medium, color, texture, composition. Not all of these exist with respect to each other on a single "axis," for the aspect of composition, for example, cross-cuts medium, color and texture. Moreover, within an aspect such as medium, we have been ambiguously referring both to material *identity* and material composition and modularity. Wall $/E/_1$ may be realized in limestone blocks, as is wall $/E/_2$; but the internal composition of the blocks—how they are laid out in courses, and the sizes of individual blocks—may contrast sharply, even if all four othe aspects remain invariant.

One thing about material structure is already abundantly clear: its orderings, or levels of organization, are considerably more complicated than the orderings manifest in formal structure. The routines comprising material structure, in other words, appear to be much more highly ordered in some sense than those of formal structure: many more aspects are involved, and their interactions seem to be highly complex.

Seen as sets of orderings, it is evident that formal structure and material structure interrelate as partially-ordered sets (posets), wherein an assymmetry of mappings is manifest. In other words, a single formal item may map onto a wide variety of alternative material "items," and, conversely, a given material item may map onto a variety of formal items.

For example, formal item /A/ (column) is invariant with respect to alternative material representations (*e.g.*, timber or stone (of a couple of varieties)); while from a material point of view, either wood or stone is invariant with respect to its mapping onto a wide variety of formal items (not only columns but walls, floors, ceilings, etc.). It is in this sense, then, that the overall sum of inter-set mappings may be termed partially-ordered: not every item in one set maps onto every item in the other set. This asymmetry is a function of series of constraints imposed both architectonically and extra-architectonically or culturally. We might imagine the situation as describing a "figure" in a conceptual space comprised of a network of all the possible mappings that could occur in architectonic systems: not all "points" in such a grid will be touched by the "figure" described for a given corpus, and corporea will be found contrastive in this respect.

Let us now try to specify the internal organization of material structure. We require at least the following aspects or components:

(1)   an inventory of materials specific to a corpus (*medium*);
(2)   a set of regulations whereby such materials are positionally related to each other (*composition*);
(3)   a further set of regulations whereby such material compositions are assigned a metric size (we may term this aspect *modularity*[a]).

In (1) we include two additional sub-routines of orderings, which we will term (a) texturization and (b) coloration. These may be seen as sub-routines of (1) in the sense that contrasts are observed in the corpus between two identical media and their physical finishing or texturing (*e.g.*, a roughly-hewn limestone block and a smoothly polished one—there may be a broad continuum between the two poles) or their coloration (note that two walls of identical media *and* texturing may be contrastively colored, and vice-versa: two walls of identical media *and* coloration may be contrastively textured or finished).

It is important to note that there may be variations within a corpus or even within a space-cell with respect to the *sequencing* of these ordering routines and sub-routines over time. Thus, a block of limestone may be inserted into a wall in a rough-hewn state resulting solely from the process of its separation from other blocks in a quarry, or it may be finished or textured in a variety of ways after it is in place in a wall. Or there may be whole sequences or "scores" of routines performed at various stages in the processing of a material from its "natural" state to its architectonic state. Moreover, such routines of *work* will be partly embedded in the requirements of the architectonic system itself and in certain conventional routines of labor—the organization of work-crews, economic or financial factors, requirements of an "aesthetic" nature, and so forth.

If so many extra- or para-architectonic factors enter into the realization of architectonic objects, how is it then possible to specify what is strictly architectonic and what is not?

We cannot specify the relative positioning of certain routines over time for a given architectonic object except insofar as evidence for this can be deduced from the appearance of the objects themselves. Moreover, identical results might be achieved by different sequencing operations—whether we put together the parts of a watch in a linear, additive sequence or if we organize the construction of the watch by a series of hierarchically-related subroutines (now the springs, now the facets, etc.), in many cases the finished results will appear identical—though the latter routines of assembly may be *faster*.[4]

Let us see how these aspects may interact by considering the realization of formal items specific to our corpus. The corpus distinguishes approximately 18 contrastive materials in the realization of its space-cells, comprising eight types of stone, treated and untreated vegetation, and a variety of media which consist of processed combinations of ecological resources. These 18 materials reveal a number of distinctions in contextual usage—certain hard stones are employed in paving, softer ones in internal flooring; certain materials have conventional associations with space-cells used for sacred *vs.* secular purposes, etc.

The inventory of materials employed in the corpus is as follows:[5]

1. marble (mrb)
2. sidheropetra (ironstone) (sdh)
3. alabaster (alb)
4. breccia (bre)
5. kouskouras (ksk)
6. gypsum (gyp)
7. sandstone (snd)
8. shist (shs)

among various types of stone; these are graded here from harder to softer (1. to 8.)

9. lime mortar (lmr)
10. pozzolana (finer concrete) (poz)
11. calcestruzzo (coarser concrete) (clc)
12. adobe brick (brk)
13. lepidha (lpd)
14. rough stucco (stc)
15. terracotta (ter)

among materials derived from a combinatory processing of stone, earth, water and vegetation; and

16. beaten earth (ear)
17. timber (mostly cypress) (tmb)
18. reeds (rds)

We shall refer to these materials by abbreviation in what follows, or, in the case of tight diagrams, by number.

It may be of interest to classify this inventory according to the interaction of its members:

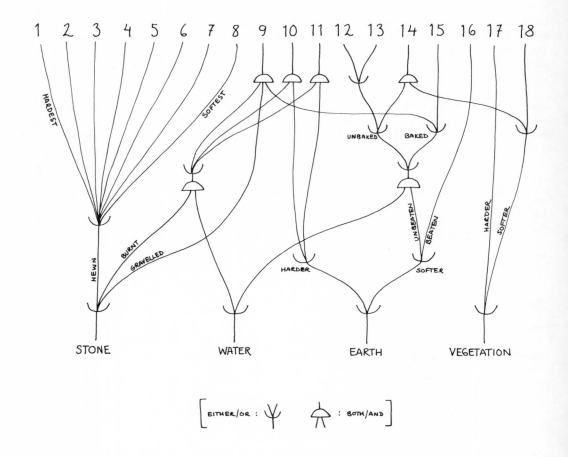

Figure 2[10]

Out of the continuum of the ecology, then, certain distinctions are made which serve as a basis of an inventory of materials employed in the realization of *forms*. This inventory represents a set of contextually-distinct variants. These distinctions, in other words, are contextually significant: i.e., a given formal configuration is realized materially as member "x" in a specific functional context, and as member "y" in a different functional context.

But this is not invariably so; a given material distinction may not be made. In other words, for example, if a given functional context—say a "pillar crypt"—is realized materially by a given material item, this occurrence may only be *characteristic* rather than universal across all examples, and we should be wary of claiming that in every stance of this functional context the same material item will always be present.

In some cases, in other words, a corpus will specify that a given cellular context *must* incorporate as a component of its organization a given material item or items, and a given material composition; but there will be cases of relatively "free" variance, where such a material item need not necessarily occur. What may be constant or invariant across the realizations of a given functional context will be *something*—but this may be a constancy of size, or orientation, or shape, or coloration, or relative position in an aggregate of cells, etc.

For example, if we look at the plans of the three major Minoan "palaces,"[6] it would appear that there is a constancy of orientation of the long axis of the central courtyards (i.e., north-south, generally). But if we also consider the orientations of the long axis of the courtyards of other palatial compounds (i.e., in addition to the major "palaces" at Knossos, Mallia and Phaistos, look at Plati, for example), then it would appear that what is constant is *not* the "north-south" orientation, but an alignment on the peak of a (religiously-significant?) mountain.[7]

In a similar fashion, we should be wary of affirming constancy or invariance in a corpus on the basis of the presence or absence of *specific items*, and look to sets of underlying relative equivalencies across various levels of organization of contexts.

In *Figure* 2. above, it will be seen that the inventory of materials arises out of a series of distinctions made on the basis of gradations of hardness-softness, treated-untreated, baked-unbaked, etc. These "features" may exist in continua *or* as binary oppositions.

Our classification distinguishes between stone, water, earth, and vegetation. This is not to assert, however, that this 4-fold distinction is itself significant in the architectonic system, *nor* that it represents a distillation of material variety such as to possibly suggest that to members of this society the world is seen as composed of (these) "four basic elements": we simply don't know, and may not ever know that much about some Minoan cosmology, or cosmologies.

Nor are we suggesting that the Minoans "had a word" for each of our 18 contextually-distinguished material items. They may not have made verbal distinctions on a one-to-one basis with these *architectonic* entities at all—or they may have had a dozen more verbal distinctions for fine gradations of limestone, though I suspect not. To be sure, what we signify by the lexical item "snow" is distinguished among various sub-Arctic peoples into many contrastive categories, according to the function of different gradations of frozen water ("x" is useful for hewing blocks for igloos, "y" for close-packing cracks between blocks, etc.).

The relationships between architectonic and lexical items are often surprisingly complex,[8] but for the moment we are not concerned with this issue. We are concerned, however, with the distinctions made within the architectonic system itself, based on significant contrasts of contextual usage: *according to the way they built* (not according to how they may have *talked about* the way they built), the Minoan corpus makes these 18 distinctions.[9]

Thus far, we have examined the inventory of materials in the corpus—its media; we will now turn to a consideration of the manner whereby certain *forms* are represented or expressed in these media.

With respect to medium, given *forms* distinguished by the corpus will be realized in a variety of materials in various contextual situations. The following diagram illustrates the set of alternative realizations of the *form* /E/ (wall). In the diagram, "i" refers to contexts where a wall is an interior partition in an aggregate of cells; "e" to contexts where a wall is an exterior wall of a cell or a cellular aggregate.

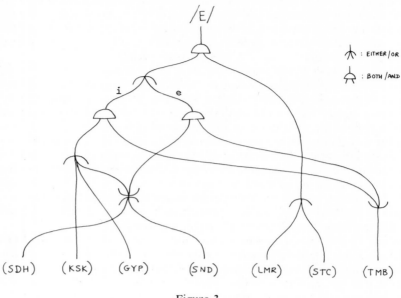

Figure 3

The set [(sdh) (ksk) (gyp) (snd) (lmr) (stc) (tmb)] may be seen as the *domain* of the mapping of /E/ onto material form, and the mapping-configuration as the material *structure* of the relationship of /E/ and this set. Different *forms* will map onto partially-contrastive domains; for example, /D/:

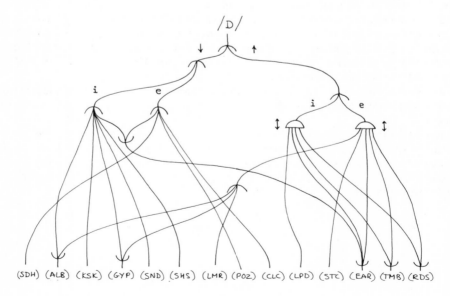

Figure 4

In the diagram, "i" and "e" are to be read as in the previous *Figure*; the arrow ↓ refers to a "floor" context; ↑ to a "ceiling" context; and the arrow ↕ refers to a mapping onto *either* ground-floor or ceiling contexts.

Hence, the domain of the mapping of /D/ onto material form is the set [(sdh) (alb) (ksk) (gyp) (snd) (shs) (lmr) (poz) (clc) - (lpd) (stc) (ear) (tmb) (rds)], representing the range of canonical realizations for the corpus.

It will be seen in both previous diagrams that in addition to the specification of alternative realizations (portrayed by divergences from the ⋀ symbol), there are general specifications of combinatory realizations (portrayed by divergences from the ⌄ symbol), or in other words, a consideration of material *composition*. It would appear possible to portray this second aspect of material 'syntax' by specifications of *ordered conjunctive*[a] relationships.[11]

Thus, /E/ is seen as realized by various stone items *as well as* (a) lime mortar (lmr) or (b) stucco (stc) applied, respectively, on interior ("i") surfaces and exterior ("e") surfaces. And in addition, timber (tmb) is employed as an interpenetrating "half-timber framework" within the composition of the various types of stone wall—in an interior context, timber is used with (ksk), (gyp) and (sdh); in exterior walls, timber is found used with either (sdh) or (snd).

Other formal items may be similarly portrayed with respect to their own contrastive realizations, but these two examples should be sufficiently illustrative of our point.

Considering, then, that the aspect of composition can be portrayed as a series of ordered conjunctive relationships—i.e., not only medium (a) + (b) + (c), but an *ordering* of these media in a tridimensional frame (such that (a) is positioned as a timber framework, (b) is a stone "infilling" of that frame, and (c) is a stucco wash over the vertical surfaces of the whole object)—then it may be possible to specify both *medium* and *composition* with the same diagrammatic notation employed in our figures. Furthermore, we can also portray *coloring* as a *marked* state of the surface organization—*vs.* an *unmarked* state wherein the natural coloration of materials is left as is; and a similar situation may be described for *texturization*.[12] But such markings are necessarily corpus-specific.

Coloration, then, may be seen as a subroutine of ordering which projects simultaneously into the given mapping of materials and composition, and may be added to or contrasted with the limemortar and stucco already part of our inventory (pigment is also, in other words, a material added to an object much as other (thicker) materials are affixed or infixed).

We might incorporate coloration into our inventory of materials in a simple way by considering that pigments are made up of combinations of natural materials—earth, vegetation, water, oils, ground stone—so that certain combinations of given materials in the inventory will generate additional members of the inventory. Such an operation would expand our inventory to cover the range of contrastive colors employed in the objects of our corpus, but the expansion would not be very great at all.

IMPLICATIONS

It will be evident in the foregoing discussions that the organization of material structure not only reveals systemic as well as sematectonic properties in terms of signification, but that it also reveals gradient as well as discrete formative features. It thereby shares with formal structure certain organizational properties with respect to the ordering of its constitutive elements.

There are found to exist relationships among these items of (1) conjunction[a] (or additive composition); (2) disjunction[a] (or alternative realization); (3) negation (existing as a constraint upon the realization of *forms* in materials); as well as (4) equivalency (wherein certain material objects exist as equivalent realizations in specifiable contexts: thus, in the mapping of /E/, items (sdh) and (snd) are equivalent realizations in "exterior" contexts).

It would seem that a similar relational geometry underlies the organizational interaction of entities in both material and formal structure. Note that, in both cases, out of a range of possible distinctions, certain ones are made which serve to establish an equilibrated network of units or items. These distinctions arise by means of the relative contrasts of certain bundles of simultaneously-occurrent features. In the case of formal structure, these features are either topological, perspectival, or geometric. In the realm of material structure, formative features comprise graded or binary-contrastive material properties (hard to soft, opaque to transparent, processed/unprocessed, etc.), and material entities are made to serve contrastively in specific contexts. In both organizational areas, the number of items is small.

In addition to an equilibrated set of items serving as systemic units, both material and formal structure reveal a set of relationships which units enter in upon with respect to each other; these are of the four *types* noted just above: conjunction, disjunction, negation, and equivalency.

Also, there is manifest in both material and formal syntax sets of regulations or constraints upon relationships between items or unities: not every item relates in the same way to every other—certain relationships, while possible in other corpora, are forbidden in ours; some relationships are possible but no examples are currently found; and some relationships are both forbidden and impossible in any corpus.

At the beginning of this section, we suggested that formal structure stands, relative to material structure, as a core series of orderings in an architectonic system behind or beneath the complex variety of realized *forms*. We have now seen that what we have come to call material structure is essentially a *structure of mappings* of formally-distinguished entities into and across aspects of medium, composition and modularity, resulting in physically-realized architectonic forms. This structure of mappings is specific to a given corpus and involves routines and sub-routines of highly complex orderings. We would suggest, moreover, that in its essential structural nature it underlies the material realization of *forms* in architectonic systems in general.

Let us now summarize these observations on the nature of material structure in an architectonic system.

Material structure will comprise

(1) an inventory of "materials" or media employed by a corpus to represent significant formal relationships. This inventory will be a subset of the resources of an ecological niche (or niches) as a society chooses to see (i.e., use) such resources. This inventory, furthermore, will comprise a relational structure of units opposed or contrasted to other units. The significance of the occurrence of given items will be simultaneously systemic or contrastive (cues, as it were, for perceptually distinguishing among formal components of a corpus), as well as sematectonic in a broad sense—the presence or absence of given aspects of material form will be intended to recall, to users of such objects, certain conventional behavioral and cognitive associations: thus, in a given built environment, the architectonic use of a certain color, or of certain kinds of materials, may by convention be associated with a certain social identity, or certain distinguished behavioral functions within a group.

(2) specified relationships among unities comprising this inventory ("composition") such that certain conjunctive and disjunctive relations are established among elements. Composition may be seen as a series of orderings among this relationally-distinguished set of unities. The material inventory, then, manifests a dimensionality in that the identity of a given element incorporates a "positionality" with respect to certain other elements in the inventory. We might envision this aspect of material structure as a geometry or figure of the conceptual space of a given inventory: not only are material items distinguished among each other, they are simultaneously distinguished among each other in a framework or grid of relationships. A given item exists, in other words, on an axis of contrast or opposition, and on an axis of positional interaction.

Included in composition is an additional aspect, namely what we have called modularity or size (or quantity), involving the translation of formal bundles of height-length-width ratios into alternative metric realizations in physical materials. Modularity concerns the realization of "composed" sets of material items—material objects which themselves are realizations of formal unities (*e.g.*, walls, columns, floors, etc.). It may be seen that there are several aspects of modularity—the specifications of materially-realized formal entities, and higher orders of modularity wherein aggregates of formal entities—whether infra-cellular or supra-cellular—are materially realized in modular arrangements—for example, in the case where all the cells in a compound are of the same size, or contrastive and/or graded sizes, or where the outer facade of a building is modulated in rhythmically-distinguished sections, whether or not those sections are coterminous with internal cellular partitioning. An example of the latter in our corpus would be the rhythmically-arranged recesses and projections in the west outer walls of the Minoan palatial compounds, which is semi-independent of the arrangement of cells within the compounds. Hence we may view modularity as a compositional mapping of formal entities at all scales (*forms*, cells, aggregates) onto physical realizations.

(3) series of regulations or constraints upon the occurrence of compositional relationships. As relationally-contrasted members of the material inventory are compositionally or relationally situated with respect to each other, the sum of such relational interactions in a given corpus will be a subset of all the possible interactions that may occur: not every material item is connectible to every other item in a given corpus, and variation will be found between corpora on this count—what is "permissible" in corpus *A* may be not permissible in corpus *B*, and so on. Material structure thus defines what will be both permissible and forbidden for a corpus with respect to the interactions of its inventory of materials.

In conclusion, we have seen that an architectonic system reveals a duality of structuring wherein its relationally-contrasted unities fall into two "structural" categories or facets of organization —what we have called *formal* organization and *material* organization.

These two sets of organization in the system manifest a semi-autonomous relationship to each other in the sense that their interactive mappings form a partially-ordered set (poset): invariant formal configurations, as we have seen, are realized alternatively and contextually as material configurations. Conversely, and asymmetrically, contrastive formal configurations may be realized in identical material compositions (which may then be seen as relatively invariant with respect to a domain of *forms*). The details of this relational invariance on both counts may be read in the mappings given above for our corpus, *Figures* 3. and 4.

However, it would appear that both of these levels of organization in an architectonic system share the same "design features" in the sense that both organizations manifest (1) sets of relationally-contrasted unities defined by the presence or absence of simultaneously-occurrent features (different types of features in both levels). Formal structure contrasts with material structure in this area in the sense that the former manifests an internally-contrastive series of organizations in three space-manifolds (geometric, perspectival, topological).

Both organizations manifest (2) conjunctive, disjunctive, negative and equivalent relationships among their contrasted elements, and (3) in both cases these relationships are constrained in terms of what a given corpus will specify as permissible or forbidden. Corpora will contrast on all three counts.

We should be wary, however, of attributing the 'duality of structure' revealed by the above to the necessary organization of the code itself. This 'duality' is principally an artifact of our analytic stance, which has focussed *sequentially* upon 'geometric' and 'material' properties of architectonic signs. Indeed, our suggestion that 'material structure' exists as a semi-autonomous network of 'mappings' between formal relationships and physical media has been metaphoric in nature, for our interest above has been to elucidate the nature of the systemic *relationships* between geometric and material sign-formations. 'Material structure' is *not* a 'surface structure' to a 'deep structure' of formal relationships. From the perspective of a given architectonic array, 'formal' and 'material' relationships are copresently manifest in syntagmatic simultaneity and sequentiality. The relationships among formal and material 'entities' in a code are discussed further in Appendix B, dealing with the network of architectonic signs.

It is evident that an architectonic system is an enormously complex system of signs of various types, and that the nature of architectonic significance is also highly complex, as we have seen in our discussion of architectonic multifunctionality. In this chapter and the previous we have attempted to portray some of the complexities of architectonic meaning as well as some of the salient features of the systemic organization of the code, its 'mechanisms', so to speak.

Both the nature of the architectonic medium and its relative signal-permanence induce significative potentials in the code which are largely unique vis-à-vis other sign systems, and contrast strikingly with verbal language. But the two systems have their own powerful advantages: while verbal language may be relatively impoverished in terms of its phonesthetic potential compared to the extraordinary multidimensional richness of the architectonic code,[13] it nevertheless offers a unique power in terms of its rapidity and effability of focus.

But we should be wary of seeing these unique systemic properties as 'deficient' in its complementary sign-system. Meaningfulness is not the privileged property of any one code, and human communication is inherently multimodal, orchestrating meaning through the intercalation of copresent signings drawn from many different sources and addressing many of our senses simultaneously.

FOOTNOTES

CHAPTER V

[1]See Preziosi, *Origins* . . . , Chapter II.

[2]See on this subject the sober remarks of A. Rapoport, *House Form and Culture*, Englewood Cliffs, New Jersey, 1969.

[3]In the sense, that is, of being related to non-architectonic factors situated elsewhere in the concerns of a society.

[4]See H. Simon, *The Sciences of the Artificial*, Cambridge, Mass., 1969, for a discussion of organizational hierarchies related to practice.

[5]See J. W. Graham, *The Palaces of Crete*, Princeton, New Jersey, 1962, 143 ff.

[6]*Ibid.*, Plates.

[7]On the question of topographical alignments of Minoan buildings, see the conjectures of V. Scully, *The Earth, the Temples and the Gods*, New Haven, 1968, second edition, incorporating the present writer's corrections.

[8]See Preziosi, 1978k.

[9]Compare B. L. Whorf, *op. cit.*, 199 ff.

[10]In the diagrams of the present chapter, the symbols used signify an additive or conjunctive relationship (closed half-circle) or a disjunctive or either/or relationship (half-circle) among items connected by lines, as explicated in the glossary below.

[11]I.e., as series of hierarchically-ordered additive relations.

[12]The question of 'markedness' is evidently an important one in architectonic systems, as it is in the linguistic system, although as yet no comprehensive study of the phenomenon has been made.

[13]Clearly, we are assuming here that the sematectonic usage of material formations in the architectonic system is generally correlative to linguistic phonological phenomena such as phonesthesia. But this is a complex problem; see R. Jakobson and L. R. Waugh, *op. cit.*, Chapter IV. The current research of Dora Vallier on architecture promises some clarification of these problems.

Chapter VI
Conclusions: The Systematicity of the Built Environment

In the words of Terence Hawkes,

> Even the most 'utilitarian' buildings organize space in various ways, and in so doing they signify, issue some kind of message about the society's priorities, its presuppositions concerning human nature, politics, economics, over and above their overt concern with the provision of shelter, entertainment, medical care, or whatever.[1]

In the present study we have attempted to indicate and describe the complexities of architectonic organization and signification. The systematic study of the built environment as a system of signs—as a semiotic system—is just beginning. But it is already evident that the architectonic code shares a number of important design features with other human sign-systems, particularly with regard to the nature of its formative processes.

It has long seemed as if this should be so, but it has not been until we had begun to analyze built environments *on their own terms*, and to situate a number of traditional questions in a systematic framework, that the various *correlative* properties of sign-systems have become more clearly apparent.

MULTIDIMENSIONALITY

The architectonic code or system of signs is a complexly-ordered device for the transmission of information regarding the cueing of the perception of identities and differences in the visual channel, decodable spatiotemporally. Architectonic formations consist of artifactual and/or appropriated environmental constructs conventionally linked to culture-specific information about the conceptual world of a society.

Generically, distinctions in formation are linked to differences in meaning. The architectonic sign comprises a copresent formal configuration and its intended conceptual domain of reference.

An architectonic formation (such as a village, building or a made pile of stones) exists spatially and temporally, in several senses. A formation is a tridimensional construct whose constitutive components may be visually palpable either piecemeal, over time, or largely copresent more or less as a totality, depending upon the position of the addressee(s). Normally, an architectonic formation is only partially copresent in the visual channel, and its totality unfolds for an addressee over time, as a result of somatotopic interaction.

It is important, moreover, to recall that vision and visual address is *directional* in nature whereas audition and vocal broadcast is *omnidirectional*. This difference is crucial to any comparative understanding of architectonic and linguistic systems, and again points up the increasingly evident fact that in so many ways, linguistic and architectonic formations dovetail, complement and supplement each other.

Architectonic formations transmit information on a continuous basis relative to other semiotic formations (verbal utterances, gestural signing, etc.), thereby maintaining a relative object-permanence. There may be a very great range in the permanence of broadcast in a given corpus: a transmission may last indefinitely long, as in the case of an Egyptian pyramid, or may be momentary and ephemeral, as with an umbrella raised in a rainstorm or an annually recurrent parade along a boulevard.

The architectonic code is not dependent upon specific kinds of physical media: the medium of the built environment consists of anything and everything drawn from the visually-palpable resources of the biosphere, from frozen blocks of water in the Arctic to wattle-and-daub to ashlar masonry, as well as place-frames constructed simply by the relative positioning of bodies. Architectonic formations are not necessarily positionally stable; they may be rolled, floated or flown away.

While architectonic formations unfold within the dimensional parameters of euclidean geometric space, they also reveal organizational properties of a topological and perspectival nature which are copresent as distinctive features with the former.

A given formation reveals structural properties which are multidimensional in a tripartite sense: (1) geometrically, with the three dimensions of euclidean space; (2) perspectivally, with the parameters of egocentric projective-planar space; and (3) topologically, with the parameters of distinctive domains, fields or loci. Thus the specification of the component properties of a formation will be a function of the geometric, perspectival and topological perspectives upon that formation. Distinctive contrastive features in one perspective may be non-distinctive or irrelevant in another perspective.

In addition, architectonic formations reveal another multidimensional parameter induced by the nature of the signalling medium: a construct may reveal alternative material realizations even where the above tripartite properties remain invariant. Thus, formal invariance may underlie material variations in color, texture, materials, metric size, and so forth. Similarly, the reverse will obtain. Generically speaking, the task of architectonic analysis will involve the elaboration of models to account for the relational invariance of structures at all levels of organization.

An architectonic transmission may often be augmented, with partial redundancy, by formative features in nonvisual channels. Thus, in a village of thatched huts a hut reserved for worship of gods or ancestors may be externally identical to all others formally (and perhaps even largely identical internally), but may be slightly different materially, incorporating materials which tinkle in the wind or which make noise when it rains in ways noticeably different from the noise made by residential huts.

In short, the analysis of architectonic communication, representation and expression must take into account every distinctive feature of organization, both materially and formally.

An important characteristic of architectonic codes is the dispensibility of artifactual formations. Architectonic signs may be replaced by correlative signs in other modalities, and by various kinds of corpus-specific symbols which with varying degrees of iconicity or indexicality stand for artifactual formations themselves, as for example where a circle of stones may replace a built hut, and so forth. Often, the given landscape itself takes on architectonic significance merely by the insertion of bodies into it, as with our circle of seated elders assembling on a meadow once a month. In many societies there will be found a great amount of code-switching between architectonic and somatotopic formations, a situation by no means confined to nomadic or hunter-gatherer peoples. Indeed, there are no groups which do not communicate architectonically as we do: there is evidently a fundamental family resemblance among the architectonic systems of all extant human groups.

THE HIERARCHY OF SIGNS

An architectonic formation consists of transmitted information carried by a variety of co-present sign types. Several kinds of architectonic signs have been identified. The primary unit in the code which is directly significative is the *space-cell*, having two alternative formal realizations: (1) a distinctive spatial configuration bounded by masses (a closed cell), and (2) a distinctive mass configuration bounded by space, which may or may not be artifactually delimited (an open cell or locus).

The space-cell enters into aggregations of cells (*matrices*) defined principally by the geometry of their tridimensional syntax or interaction. In a given corpus, certain habitual matrices may occur like stock phrases, but in general the matrix as an architectonic sign consists of an abstract diagram of arrangements which may have a wide variety of formal and material realizations. Essentially, at this level of organization the focus of analysis is upon the relative arrangements of other signs (cells).

Larger communicative unities comprise conventional, and even more abstract or diagrammatic, relative arrangements of matrices into neighborhoods, settlements, and so forth. It will be clear that a settlement need not comprise large aggregates of cells or cell-matrices, but may consist of a single cell (open or closed).

The architectonic code is built upon a principle of duality or double articulation. The 'smallest' directly-significative unit in a code, the space-cell, is built out of sign-units which are not directly significative in themselves, but are rather systemically-significant. Such *forms* function principally in a sense-discriminative manner to distinguish one cell from another, and are meaningful primarily in this sense. (See Appendix B below.)

In given corpora, forms may also serve sense-determinative functions as in cases where a given facade or cell-component is directly significative of a certain conceptual domain.

In a parallel sense, the material realizations of architectonic formations may serve a dual significative role: on the one hand they reveal a systemic function to discriminate one form from another in perceptually-palpable ways, and on the other hand they may take on sense-determinative or sematectonic roles. An example of the latter would be a case where the material articulation of a given form is conventionally associated with certain cultural meanings. Thus, cells painted crimson, or built of ashlar limestone, or twice the size of other cells in a settlement, may be canonically associated with a ruling class in contrastive opposition to cells associated with an underclass, cued by cells painted blue (or anything *but* crimson, mudbrick construction, or half the size (or generically smaller than) the former.

The identification of signs in a corpus is corpus-specific; what are significative unities in one system may be non-significant or non-present in another system. The set of distinctive *forms* of corpus W will differ from that of corpus X, as will the set of possible *cells* and the range of cell-*matrices*. Moreover, two apparently identical formations (both materially and formally) in two different corpora will normally be contrastively meaningful (homonymy), as members of distinct architectonic systems.

Architectonic forms comprise sets of copresent spatial *features* which distinguish one form from another, and serve to define components of the set of forms, which is finite in extent. While there exists a generic correlativity between architectonic and linguistic distinctive features in a *systemic* sense, architectonic spatial features are quite unique in their properties. Moreover, the latter are distinguished by being tripartitely organized. There exist three classes of architectonic features: geometric, perspectival or planar, and topological.

Geometric features of a form consist of relative ratios within a ternary space-manifold (height, length, width) such that forms in a corpus are conventionally contrastively opposed to each other. Thus, form G is distinguished from form H on the basis of its geometric features: (2:1:1) vs. (3:2:1).

Forms are also distinguished from each other in a planar or perspectival sense, involving egocentric parameters. Thus, the same form (as a tridimensional geometric construct) may have different planar features relative to the parameters of the visual channel, depending, in other words, on its cellular position (above vs. below; in front of vs. in back of; to the right of vs. to the left of).

From a topological perspective, distinctions in either planar or formal formation may become neutralized or non-relevant, just as from a planar perspective various disjunctions in form may be non-relevant. Topological features involve bounded unicums: from this point of view, a cell is defined as a formation with a property of boundedness which remains invariant over a variety of formal and planar transformations.

An architectonic code comprises a hierarchical ordering of sign types in the following manner:

    (a) features: formal / planar / topological
    (b) systemic units: forms / planes / domains
    (c) directly significative units: cells
    (d) aggregates of units: matrices

Normally, the 'largest' sign type to be coded as such in a system is the cell; 'above' the level of the cell, architectonic signs consist of patterns (coded as such).

A built environment is a complex spatiotemporal framework for human action and interaction whose components are less like building blocks and more like patterns of potential signification; its structure is not to be found as a definite arrangement of constituent parts, but is given by sets of interrelationships, less of *things* and more of *choices* among formations. The components of an architectonic formation can only be understood in terms of their interactions with the rest of that formation, in the context of that formation's associations with others in a *system* of formations.

Architectonic objects comprise patterned, multidimensional arrangements of forms articulated by means of rule-governed oppositions between masses and spaces unfolding for the addressee(s) over space and time. The 'vocabulary' of the built environment consists of elements formed by perceptually palpable edges, boundaries and other discontinuities in formation. Such elements acquire significance less in terms of their inherent properties and more in terms of their relationships to other items in multidimensional arrays.

The primary directly-significative unit in an architectonic code, the space-cell, is 'built up' out of forms, planes and domains, themselves distinguished by sense-discriminative geometric, perspectival and topological features. It has been noted that the cell may consist of spatial configurations bounded by mass (closed cell) or massive configurations bounded by space (open cell). What is common to these alternative formal realizations is a perceptually-palpable *alternation* between mass and space, a binary-contrastive opposition. Necessarily, this is not an opposition analogous to 'sound-and-silence', for an architectonic code consists of distinctive configurations in both mass and space. There are no 'empty' spaces in a settlement from an architectonic point of view. Corpora are contrasted with each other on the basis of distinctive spatial conformations as well as distinctive mass conformations.

A space cell is defined by means of this particular kind of alternative patterning, which is *systemically* correlative in a generic sense to the alternative patterning of the (albeit more simply unlinear) consonantal/vocalic conformations of a linguistic code. In both codes, this kind of alternative patterning provides an essential template for perception. In the architectonic code, this patterning is inherently more complex, being multidimensional in its parameters. An architectonic space is no more the 'absence' of mass than mass is the 'absence' of space.

MULTIFUNCTIONALITY

In the architectonic code, as in any semiotic system, the meaningfulness of a formation is dependent upon a variety of functional factors according to the particular orientation of that formation toward one or another of the constituent elements of any semiotic transmission.

A given architectonic formation normally reveals more than one function, and invokes different aspects of meaningfulness at the same time. The 'function' of an architectonic object—in the sense of its contextual reference or behavioral usage—is but one of six copresent architectonic functions, which are generically shared with other semiotic systems. In architectonic semiosis, an orientation upon

(1)	'usage' or semantic context	=	the referential function;
(2)	the formation itself	=	the aesthetic function;
(3)	the code of system	=	the meta-codal or allusory function;
(4)	maintenance of contact	=	the phatic or territorial function;
(5)	the 'addresser'	=	the emotive or expressive function;
(6)	the 'addressee'	=	the conative function.

Any given architectonic formation will reveal the copresence of these functional horizons in varying degrees of dominance. The first four of these horizons were perceived clearly by the Czech theoretician J. Mukařovský in his 1938 paper on architectural function, and in this regard his observations appear to have been inspired by contemporary linguistic research, notably that of Jakobson (reported more recently in 1956).[2]

Several factors within architectonic semiosis induce significant distinctions between the horizons of addresser and addressee in comparison with the linguistic code, and it is on these horizons that the former writer reveals a certain unclarity.

It is necessary to stress the role played in architectonic transmission by its peculiar medium and by the permanence of its signalling. The very fact that architectonic formations remain in the visual channel and continually broadcast induces a situation which is more complex than what obtains normally in linguistic semiosis. A linguistic utterance is (unless translated into optical representations) momentary and ephemeral. A plethora of speech acts may exist against the ground of a single architectonic broadcast. The idealized 'speaker-hearer' of verbal language finds an occasional correlate on the architectonic side, but this is not normally the case.

Furthermore, in the architectonic code, the original generator of a formation may be a person or persons who 'design' an object, who may also (but need not) 'build' that formation for a 'client' (who may be the generator or builder) who employs that formation significantly, thus serving as a transmitter of that signal to himself (or to themselves) or to others, or to both.

An additional comparative difference must be taken into account. In linguistic transmission, a speaker or addresser produces acoustic signals through the instrumentality of his own vocal organs, to be decoded by an addressee or hearer with his own auditory organs. In architectonic semiosis, the correlative addresser generates sign-formations through the instrumentality of his limbs and body (somatotopically) or by means of surrogate instrumentalities (tools, machines, and so forth), to be decoded by addressees with their own visual organs, employed directionally through spatiokinesis.

But in an architectonic code, the principal addresser is the user of a formation (whether he or she generated or built the sign-formation himself or not), and, furthermore, a sign-formation may have many users, a concomitant of the relative object-permanence of architectonic signals. Buildings remain in the visual channel to be continually used and intersubjectively appropriated; sentences do not.

Consequently, the architectonic addresser may (or may not) stand at the temporal end of a chain comprising designers and builders, but *his semiotic position is correlative to that of a linguistic speaker*. Thus, the former may employ a given sign formation (with or without infrastructural or exoskeletal modifications) in such a way as to emphasize the user's attitude toward what he is using, and such an orientation is correlative to the emotive function in verbal language.

In a similar fashion, the organization of a formation with an orientation upon addressees (conation) finds an architectonic correlate in the somatotopic constraints offered by an object in terms of the prescription of various kinds of movement, passage, and spatial activity of any kind, and in particular upon various kinds of prescribed activity. One may be exhorted not to go down the up staircase through a variety of formal and material means, including everything from physical constraints upon movement to arrows, diagrams and even optical representations of verbal messages. Ariadne's thread and the traffic signal on the corner both participate in architectonic conation.

Clearly, the understanding of architectonic functionality has had a long and confused history, and the spurious question as to whether 'architecture' (itself, as we have insisted, only a portion of the architectonic system) is 'art', craft, engineering, theatre, or housing is best laid to rest. Much received analysis has suffered from a misconstrual of architectonic functionality wherein attention has been given principally to two functions—namely the contextually-referential or usage function, and the aesthetic function.

The built environment is no more an 'art' than its sociocultural complement and supplement, verbal language, except insofar as a given formation may reveal a dominance of orientation upon the formation itself for its own sake—correlative to the 'poetic' function of verbal language.

Much of the confusion regarding architectonic function stemmed from a misconstrual of the aesthetic function with given and necessary object-types, a result of culture-bound prejudice analogous to a situation in verbal language where at a given place and time certain vocabularies were deemed more 'poetic' than others. This is also in part the result of a confusion between the characteristic dominance of an aesthetic orientation accruing to certain kinds of architectonic formations in various familiar Western corpora—such as churches and palaces—which tend toward a certain stability and continuity. It need not be stressed that the aesthetic function is autonomous of given object or usage types.

The aesthetic function of architectonic objects is often confused with their meta-codal or allusory function, wherein a formation reveals a predominant orientation upon the code itself in its historicity. Thus, a trolley-barn built to resemble an Ostian apartment block alludes to a known corpus of formations and provides a certain commentary upon it, while at the same time calling attention to itself as a formation.

It cannot be overstressed that architectonic formations are multifunctional in their very nature, revealing the copresence of a variety of orientations upon the different components in any transmission. It may be doubted that single-function formations exist. There will be observed a dominance of a given function over others in a given formation, held in dynamic equilibrium by the coeval set of currently subordinate functions. Moreover, it must be stressed that such functionality changes over time within the 'same' formation, so that it is necessary in architectonic analysis to speak of a diachronic variability with respect to function. A building put up in the Seicento as a palazzo converted in the Novecento to government offices and reconverted recently as a memorial to unknown soldiers is more than the 'same' building with different usages; these are three different semiotic formations.

The property of object permanence relative to somatotopic and linguistic signing induces a hitherto little-explored dimension to semiotic study, namely a concern with communicative *events per se* in their multimodal totality. Whereas generically speaking an architectonic formation remains relatively invariant across a variety of linguistic and somatotopic signings, from the perspective of the communicative event in its totality, the multimodal message contains distinctive elements in the latter two modalities at different times. Consequently, the meaningfulness of an architectonic formation will be in part a function of its *embeddedness in copresent signings* —in other words, in a network of signs drawn from several modalities or codes.

Such a situation is correlative to that obtaining in any transmission in any code wherein the same formation acquires contextually-variant meanings depending upon its syntactic surround. Humans respond to a combination of stimuli across chemical, tactile, acoustic and visual modalities, and in many cases across all four. Speech acts are cooccurrent with signals in a variety of other modalities, and the meaningfulness of an utterance represents only a portion of the total meaning of a communicative *event*. The analysis of transmissions in any one modality may not necessarily result in an entirely complete or coherent message. Much of the information simultaneously broadcast may be redundant (i.e., perceptually enhanced) and augmentative. Some of it may be contradictory or modifying.

A semiotics of communicative events in their characteristically normal multimodality has yet to be born, and it is clearly in this direction that an important part of the future of semiotics lies. We need to know how the various sign systems employed by humans are designed to function in concert with each other.

In the ongoing semiotic bricolage of daily life, humans will employ anything and everything at their disposal to communicate information, from pan-human codes such as verbal language, somatotopic signing and architectonic structuration to transitory ephemera arising as transformations of transformations.

The many different sign systems evolved by humans are not all different ways of doing the same things; each modality offers its own partly-unique advantages under the shifting conditions or social life. But each symbol system is not entirely unique either structurally or functionally; there is a great deal of necessary overlapping among systems, and each is complexly cross-indexed with the other and all are deictically interlinked.[3]

The more we understand the particular parameters of organization of nonverbal codes such as the architectonic system, the less will we be inclined to view the position of verbal language as an active semiotic figure against a static and passive ground. Concomitantly, we shall be in a better position to understand how and why each system provides its own particularly powerful perspective on the totalities of human experience, and the ways in which each such perspective necessarily implicates all others. In this regard, architectonic inquiry provides the potentially richest frontier for the growth and maturity of our understanding of the human orchestration of meaning.

No attempt at a comprehensive semiotics of the built environment can, at this stage in its development, be final. This is no less true of the present study, whose chief function has been to define the proper questions to be asked.

FOOTNOTES

CHAPTER VI

[1]Terence Hawkes, *Semiotics and Structuralism*, Berkeley, California, 1977, 134.

[2]J. Mukařovský, *op. cit.*, 236 ff; R. Jakobson, "Metalanguage as a Linguistic Problem," Presidential Address to the Linguistics Society of America, December 27, 1956, and "Linguistics and Poetics," in T. Sebeok, ed., *Style in Language*, 1960, 350-377.

[3]The subject of *deixis* is one of the most important questions in linguistic analysis as well as of prime concern in the study of architectonic meaning. See the writer's forthcoming monograph, "Multimodal Communication," 1978k, and see Appendix A.

Appendix A
The Multimodality
of Communicative Events

In the semiotic task of revealing more precisely the *place* of the built environment—or any other system of signs—in communication, the analysis of *communicative events* in their multi-modal totality has acquired today a fundamental urgency and importance. In the present section I would like to discuss the complexities inherent in such events as well as our current abilities to adequately model such complexities.

Communication, in the broadest sense, involves the transmission of information regarding the perception of similarities and differences. Any semiotic system is a complexly-ordered device for the cueing of such perceptions in given sensory channels and in conventionally-delimited media.

A communicative act such as a verbal utterance does not normally exist *in vacuuo* (except perhaps in the fictitious atmosphere of certain recently fashionable linguistic models); rather, speech acts are invariably co-occurrent with communicative acts in distinct signalling media. This state of affairs is neither accidental or circumstantial, for on the basis of internal evidence alone, it is increasingly evident that each of the isolable sign systems evolved by humans has been designed from the outset to function both semi-autonomously and in deictic concert with other sign systems.

But beyond an understanding of certain formative entities in the linguistic code—whose meaningfulness, as in the case of 'shifters', can only be disambiguated through cross-modal indexing—we remain at a serious loss to account for the extraordinarily complex systematicities of normal (i.e., multimodal) communication in daily life.

It has been clear for a long time that an adequate account of communicative events demands of us more than a mechanical summation of the organizational properties of particular codes as analytically isolable, and more than is currently offered by the hybrid heuristics of sociolinguistics and 'pragmatics', which, while admirable for their remarkable rediscovery of the wider world in which verbal language is embedded, nevertheless rarely escape an implicit verbocentrism. One can only stretch paralinguistics so far.

In the ongoing semiotic bricolage of daily life, we orchestrate and intercalate anything and everything at our disposal to create and maintain a significant world, or simply to get a message across. It is clear that the attempt to understand such complexities through the scientistic super-imposition of design features, analytic methods and even data language drawn from the study of one of its embedded components—for example verbal language—upon other significative modalities has, by and large, been a failure. While it is true that much has been learned by such activity, it must be decisively admitted that the ultimate expected illumination has tended to be rather dim and fleeting in comparison to the energies expended—or, as more often has happened, the mute stones and gestures have remained mute.

Of course this is not to deny the importance and relevance of a semiotics of the code—whether architectonic, gustatory, linguistic, or somatotopic; rather it becomes increasingly urgent to reaffirm the status of such models as selective, partial and synechdochal fictions.

If we are to augment the ongoing multiplication of semiotic models of specific codes in given cultural contexts beyond the trivial reductionisms of currently available 'semiotics of culture', our focus must be held tenaciously upon the actualities of semiosis in daily life which implicate and combine varieties of significative formations drawn from distinct signalling media. Moreover, general sign theory itself must push beyond the ultimate propositional logics which, perhaps not so curiously, seem to privilege the perspective (verbal or visual) of the given analyst.

None of this criticism is particularly new or original. It is raised again, and must be continued, until our picture of the extraordinarily complex nature of normal human semiosis begins to be clarified in a non-trivial fashion. Clearly, this is not intended as an indictment of the semiotic enterprise itself, rather only its dominant priorities. If semiotics is to realize its potential as a principled, insightful and radical contribution to the problem of meaning in human life, it must remain absolutely clear about the relative urgencies of its priorities.

Additionally, if semiotics is to be more than merely a new formalism, I think that we must be prepared to admit that it may be at least theoretically possible for semiotics to learn from the experience of other perspectives which in the past or at present have attempted to wrestle with equivalent problems. There is nothing more vacuous than a semiotics of art (for example) which is less well-informed or insightful than the received art history.

Again, I think these issues are self-evident, and rather than continue to persue them in the abstract, I would like to begin to address the question of the implications of a holistic and multi-modal approach to semiosis.

It is clear that communicative acts in a given medium are normally co-occurrent with acts in other modalities which may or may not implicate or address distinct sensory channels, and I think it is also clear that communicative events resemble complex, dynamically equilibrated spatiotemporal arrays of such acts, of which the basic primate display is a simple, but (in the human line) radically apotheosized analogue.

Furthermore, it is evident that the analysis of transmissions in any one of a series of copresent modalities in a communicative event may not necessarily result in an entirely complete, coherent, or homogeneous semantic domain. Much of the information simultaneously broadcast is often redundant and perceptually augmentative, and some of it may be contradictory. Some of it may be supplementary in providing collocational semantic markings with respect to information in another modality.

I think it is a reasonable assumption that each of the various sign systems employed by humans in social communication has been designed or evolved to operate in concert with all others. Cross-modal indexing, redundancy, complementarity, and supplementarity are properties of any code, perhaps to a greater degree than we may have been willing to admit in the past. Any human sign system is *de facto* not merely an open system, but is an asymmetrical and dynamic system: it possesses both dynamism in its synchronicity and stability in its diachrony.

This is an extremely complex state of affairs, since it situates human sign systems somewhere between mechanistic well-formedness and idiosyncratic bricolage; but I will also take it as a reasonable assumption that this state of affairs has not only been highly adaptive in the evolution of the human line, but that it has, in a variety of imaginable ways, been responsible for what it is we have become as a species.

The peculiar internal nature of human sign systems is both a concomitant of and a contributor to our characteristically cross-modal behavior. Moreover, the human grade of intelligence is such that when faced with a choice, we invent a third possibility, or we answer a question with a question. We contrast with our nearest primate relatives not merely by the possession of any one code (whether verbal or visual), but rather by the globality of our intelligence in all modalities.

The chief task of semiotics—its highest priority—is the clarification of the multidimensional geometries of relationship underlying this multimodal behavior, which is manifest in even the most simple communicative events in daily life. The question is, what is minimally implicated in any such event?

If we situate ourselves at the locus of verbal language, it will be evident that any speech act is co-occurrent, minimally, with the following:

(1) some state of gestural, somatotopic or spatiokinetic signing, involving the significative use of the body and its culturally and conventionally-delimited components;

(2) some state of costuming or dermal patterning, involving the significative use of artifactual markings or materials which figure a body's topologically-defined ground; and

(3) some state of architectonic or environmental structuration, involving the significative use of a built environment or an appropriated topography.

Each of these modalities—which, depending upon the conventions of a given culture, may themselves incorporate more than one 'code' as such—may be said to broadcast simultaneously with a particular speech act. In concert, these intercalated transmissions define and delimit a communicative event.

As important as it may be to identify and define the modal components of a given communicative event, it is no less important to stress and explicate their salient contrastive structural properties, for it is not the case that we are dealing with topologically identical cells in a matrix, or merely different shapes in a jigsaw puzzle. Nor for that matter will the relative contributions of copresent signings in different modalities necessarily be equivalent; nor will it be necessarily the case that they will always be hierarchicalized in any one linear direction, wherein any one set of signings invariably stands as a 'figure' to the 'ground' of other signings in other modalities.

There are significant structural differences among the copresent signings in a communicative event, which in large part are concomitants of the particular sensory channels implicated in a transmission. Vision is directional; audition is omnidirectional. Moreover, there are important differences with respect to relative permanence of broadcast: speech signals decay instantaneously; buildings and their infrastructures remain perceptually available for use across a multitude of different speech acts. Clearly, there is an ascending scale of relative 'object-permanence' is the list of modalities given above.

Thus, any nontrivial understanding of the inherent multimodality of communicative events must reject a simple summation or commutative relationship of its components, for we are dealing with different kinds of components which have been evolved to do partially different things.

The cases where a speech act occurs outside this multimodal context are relatively minimal. But the situation is not necessarily symmetrical with other modalities, and speech acts may be absent in communicative events, whether or not they are replaced by surrogate or complementary signings in other modalities. Various kinds of gestural signings may serve in such a capacity, whether derived metaphorically or synechdochally from verbal structure, or arising independently of a linguistic code. Some such systems may be truly 'deponent', in the sense of being ancillary or paralinguistic, operating in rhythmic synchrony with speech, while others will be capable of semantic disambiguation without the copresence of verbal transmission.

There is an enormous amount of redundancy in even the simplest communicative event, and a great deal of redundancy is built into the operant behavior of any code. But this phenomena is not only infra-modal, it is cross-modal, and information supplied by one modality may be augmented by distinct formations in other codes. It may well be that the particular effability of any one code is to a certain degree a concomitant of its embeddedness in arrays of copresent codes, both actually and potentially. In visual communication, the symbolic and significative potential of a given gestalt is a necessary coefficient of its ground, in mutual reciprocity. From the perspective of communicative events, this codeterminate 'ground' involves both inframodal and cross-modal contextualization.

The real question here is the extent to which we are capable of modelling such complexities. Taking merely the four modal activities noted above—namely, verbal utterances, dermal patterning, somatotopic signing, and architectonic appropriation—then our task will be to clarify the relationships defined by the operant behaviors of copresent signings in these domains. It seems evident that these relationships will not only be linearly syntagmatic, metonymical or commutative—since however useful it may be to model such phenomena as if they were 'texts' or complicated 'rebuses', they are more than these. Nor are they merely paradigmatically associated, or metaphorically related: a communicative event is necessarily more complex than a linguistic unit such as a phoneme, defined by the intersective copresence of a simultaneous bundle of distinctive features.

The relationships in question will be both metonymical or synechdochal, and metaphorical—that is to say, both syntagmatic and paradigmatic. Furthermore, whether a given relationship between signings in any two modalities is paradigmatic or syntagmatic may well be a function of the stance of the analysis. In other words, the relationship may be non-transitive or irreversible: a metaphorical relationship from one direction may be synechdochal when modelled from the other direction. All of this may be over and above the patent syntagmatic-paradigmatic oscillation among units in a particular code at different levels in its hierarchy of sign formations. It may very well be the case that not only will such relationships be asymmetrical, they may be differently asymmetrical from the standpoint of different modalities.

But there are two further complications. The first concerns the phenomenon of markedness which pervades any code: to what extent do we really understand markedness relations as applied cross-modality? I am not aware of any study which addresses this problem either directly or indirectly, although the work on palaeolithic symbol systems by the Soviet writer Toporov[1] and the American anthropologist Marshack[2] may lead to insights into this problem. It is most clearly understood in work in linguistic semiotics, notably in the work of Jakobson and others,[3] where its relationship to metaphor and metonymy is distinctly specified.

The second complication regarding the nature of cross-modal relationships in communicative events has to do with the problem of the relative dominance of various functions in a transmission in a given signing, and its copresent associations in other modalities. In other words, will it necessarily be the case that a focus upon conative, or phatic, or aesthetic functions in a given signing will be equilibrated with an equivalent focus in another modality? I suspect that here also the situational possibilities are quite complex, for it is evident that from the perspective of a communicative event in its totality, distinct modalities may contribute different weightings in functional dominance: otherwise equivalent verbal utterances with a dominance on one function may acquire different transmissive foci in different settings. Once again, this fact suggests that a semiotics of the code *per se* is a selective fiction in isolation from its multimodal communicative context. And taken together, the various complexities just outlined suggest that the relationship between a semiotics of the code and general sign theory is necessarily not metaphorical, but inevitably synechdochal.

The calibration of these possible geometries of relationship is precisely what is the most urgent task facing semiotics. As it is, it is exceedingly complex in merely dealing with the four modal domains abstractly and generically discussed here, let alone in the actual pluralistic conditions of semiosis in daily life, which involves the intercalation of signings drawn from many distinct codes,—both those inherited from our palaeolithic past, such as verbal language and the architectonic code (the latter of which is now evidenced as early as 300,000 B.C. in its present form), as well as those assembled yesterday.

The situation is precisely this: if it is the case that each of the various semiotic codes evolved by humans are irreducible with respect to each other—in other words, that the contents expressed by complex nonverbal units cannot be translated into one or more verbal units, and vice-versa, except by weak approximation— then the hope to find some uniformitarian common denominator, some 'meta' language, some non-trivial and non-reductionist general theory of semiosis, is an illusion except as a selective and synechdochal fiction. There are no metalanguages; rather (and much more interestingly) only selective infralanguages which are part and parcel of given codes. And since any infralanguage by its very nature adds to the body of a given code itself, and thereby alters its topology, so in any attempt to see itself as an object it must undoubtedly act so as to make itself distinct from, and thereby false to, itself. In this condition it will always partially elude itself. The kitten will always chase its own tail.

I suspect it is in the very nature of any human sign system to partially elude itself, and herein lies the very effability of the semiotic codes which we have evolved. But if there is no truly synoptic picture of semiosis in a value-neutral sense, no one perspective which subsumes all others, we are left with something which in the long run is inherently much more useful—namely a mutable focus on communicative events which affords a temporal and syntagmatic cascade of perspectives which selectively illuminate a situation in a stereoscopic and overlapping fashion.

It is precisely the operant nature of our multimodal understanding which privileges each perspective selectively and successively. Since any analysis is a function of the purposes to which it is put, it is in the nature of any analysis to be provisional, for there are many different functions and purposes, some of which are contradictory and irreducible, even if they may be copresent in the same analysis to varying degrees of dominance.

Consequently, it will be necessary to be explicit regarding the inevitable teleological determinants in any semiotic analysis, even if this implies not only an abandonment of a semiotics of the code except as a provisional fiction, but also an abandonment of a uniformitarian theory of semiosis itself in favor of a holographically-overlapped matrix of generic and irreducible semiotic theories.

Of course this is not to deny the necessary operational paradox that any code can be employed, in communication, as a *provisional* metalanguage. Nor is it to deny the evident fact that even though many codes are mutually irreducible in a strict sense, they may reveal correlative processes of formation and transmission, as we have argued in the present study. But whatever they share is shared by virtue of their status as human sign systems with partly-overlapping and mutually-implicative functions. Codes are necessarily correlative rather than isomorphic. The role of semiotics is to provide a clearer understanding of how and why each copresent system provides its own particularly powerful perspective on the totalities of human experience, and the ways in which each such perspective necessarily implicates all others. The most urgent task awaiting semiotics is precisely a principled attention to the directional geometries of this implication.

And in addressing these implicational relationships our analyses will be most productive when the essential and fundamental difference between meaning and reference are clearly borne in mind. Meaning is the specification of an ordered trace of relationships which a given sign or matrix of signs prescribes with respect to other signs within the same code, whereas reference is not an indexical relationship which a given sign bears to formations outside of semiotic systems, toward some fictive 'real' world, but rather involves cross-modal implications. In verbal language, for example, 'shifters' are cross-modally indexical with respect to significative formations in a somatotopic modality (i.e., the relative placements and perspectival positionings of addressers and addressees in communicative events). In an identical fashion, the 'meaning' of a given painting or environmental construct is internal to its own code, whereas the 'reference' of a mediaeval religious composition (or any other) may implicate a culturally copresent set of texts, doctrines or beliefs, which themselves comprise significative formations in their own right in adjacent codes. And the relationships among all these may be metonymic or indexical, or metaphoric.

I believe strongly that a clarification of these issues can only lead to a salient enhancement of the semiotic enterprise, shunting our focus more tenaciously upon the nature of *relationship* itself, which after all is what semiotics is all about, from its conceptual foundations to the fine grain of its ongoing analyses. I have tried to suggest here that the most productive direction such analyses can take today is in the direction of the disambiguation of the cross-modal relationships manifest in their totality primarily in the complexities of communicative events. In addition, it is only in this way that our understanding of the internal structural nature of individual codes can be made less fictive.

FOOTNOTES

[1]See N. Toporov, "Toward the Origin of Certain Poetic Symbols: the Palaeolithic Period" in H. Baran, ed., *Semiotics & Structuralism: Readings from the Soviet Union* (New York, 1976), 184-225.

[2]See A. Marshack, "Some Implications of the Palaeolithic Symbolic Evidence for the Origin of Language," in S. R. Harnad, H. D. Steklis and J. Lancaster, eds., *Origins & Evolution of Language & Speech*, New York Academy of Sciences, Volume 280 (1976), 289-311.

[3]See especially Roman Jakobson and Linda Waugh, *The Sound Shape of Language* (forthcoming 1979, Indiana University Press).

Appendix B
The Network
of Architectonic Signs

The apparent 'duality' of structure observed in the text—the 'disjunction' between 'formal' and 'material' structure in the architectonic code—is an artifact of our initial analytic stance, which focused sequentially upon the geometric and material invariants in the corpus examined. It does not correspond to a 'duality of structure' intrinsic to the network of signs itself.

Indeed, it has been implicit in our analyses of the invariant formal geometric properties of the matrix of cells comprising the 'Minoan Hall System' that a full picture of its organization necessarily incorporates certain invariant relationships among 'material' entities as well. Any given matrix is a tridimensionally-syntagmatic aggregation of cells, mass and space forms, certain materials in characteristic compositional relationships, patterns of color and texture, as well as relative size ratios among all of these entities. The organization of any such formation thus involves the syntagmatic copresence of a wide variety of sign types as these are defined by a given code.

In our analyses we made a case for the existence of two *types* of architectonic signs: those with *direct* signification and those whose signification was *indirect* or systemic. We also pointed to the evident fact that under certain conditions indirectly-significant signs may exhibit a tendency toward direct (sematectonic) signification. The same features employed as distinctive (sense-discriminative) in a given code may, under certain conditions, and for certain users, function in a directly-significative (sense-determinative) fashion: recall our discussion in Chapter II regarding distinctive, redundant, configurative, and expressive features.

The question is thereby raised concerning the nature of the *minimal* directly-significative signs in the architectonic code. We have noted that the 'largest' directly-significative sign encoded as much in the system is the *cell* (and we saw that 'above' the 'level' of the *cell, signantia* comprise *patterns* of syntagmatic aggregation—*matrices*, structures, settlements, etc.). What, then, are the 'smallest' or minimal sense-determinative sign units in a code?

The answer, from the point of view of the *signans*, is necessarily multiple: the minimally-(directly) significative units in the code may be *features* or bundles of features (*forms*), both of a 'formal' (geometric) or 'material' nature. Moreover, some such features may themselves also function in sense-discriminative ways. In other words, certain features may function, in a given code, in a sense-discriminative manner, while some of these, plus other features (i.e., redundant, configurative and expressive), will function in sense-determinative ways. The same will hold for *forms* (syntagmatically-simultaneous clusters of features).

We shall term such minimal signs *figures*, and note that their *signantia* may be quite various: geometric relationships or conformations, patterned relationships among spatial features, colors, textures, relationships of size and scale, as well as syntagmatic clusters of any of these.

Considered in this fashion, the *figure*, as the minimal directly-significative sign unit in the code, may be seen as *systemically* or operationally equivalent to the linguistic 'morpheme' if the latter is considered as a relational (rather than atomistic) entity.

It becomes increasingly evident that the architectonic and linguistic codes share correlativities of systemic organization at fundamental levels—that, in other words, they operate systemically according to equivalent design principles. This correlativity, which extends to the concept of 'double articulation'—and, to a remarkable extent, to the dynamically patterned network or hierarchy of signs themselves—is based upon a *relational* rather than atomistic or formalistic picture of both codes. In other words, it is only through a consideration of either code as a system of relationships, in which meaningfulness implicates every level of organization, that such correlativities of design become patent. Moreover, it has become clear in our study that 'form' does not exist apart from 'content': both the built environment and verbal language are systems of *signs* at all scales of organization.

In the architectonic code there exists another structural design feature which is closely paralleled in verbal language. This is the syntagmatically-sequential arrangement of *forms* and form-clusters alternatively manifesting mass and space *features*. In other words, there exists an *alternative patterning* of mass and space *forms*, a necessary concomitant of the nature of an array's sensory address. This property is patently correlative to the syntagmatic structural template involving the alternation of 'consonantal' and 'vocalic' phonemes or phoneme-clusters in language. This syllabic matrix upon which phonemes are necessarily arranged is a concomitant of the nature of acoustic perception. In both codes, this patterning is sense-discriminative in nature.

In the built environment, alternative patterning is considerably more complex, being tridimensionally (and spatiotemporally) syntagmatic, whereas in language alternative patterning is necessarily unilinear and temporal. In both cases, this structural property is a function of the mechanisms of sensory address, wherein disjunctions and gradiencies of formation exist as cues for the perception of distinctions in meaning.

While it is with a good deal of sensitivity and delicacy that any sketch of specific parallelisms among codes should be made, the results of our study, augmented by ongoing analyses parallel and subsequent to the present text, indicate forcefully that the architectonic and linguistic codes are designed along correlative lines. This is by no means to claim, however, that one is simply a cross-modal transform of the other, nor is it to assert that they are completely parallel codes in distinct media (see our remarks above in Appendix A).

The revealed correlativities of formative process, moreover, are not due to a derivative or genaeological relationship between the two systems, wherein either serves, phylogenetically or ontogenetically, as the model for the other: the architectonic code is no more built upon language than language is built upon architecture. Neither is a 'secondary modelling system' with respect to the other. Claims to this effect (in either direction) cannot be substantiated, nor forced by rhetorical fiat.

While it is patent that some semiotic systems in culture may in fact be deponent with respect to another or others, language and the built environment are panhuman sign systems which have evolved in close concert with each other from early palaeolithic times. Direct architectonic evidence—*viz.*, evidence for architectonic formations essentially identical to our own—is at least a third of a million years old. While it remains unclear to what extent verbal language as we currently have it formed a necessary component of such environments, it is a reasonable assumption that the linguistic code in something like its known form should have been copresent. For a variety of reasons, each is unthinkable without the other, and it is patent that each is designed to operate in deictic and multimodal concert with the other.

At any rate, we should be wary of confusing their operant, profound and necessary interpermeability with genaeological evidence in either direction. Indeed, any equivalencies of organization are principally due to a shared semiotic and cognitive base in which each is deeply grounded.

* * * *

The foregoing observations, taken together with the results of our analyses in the text, suggest the following picture of the structure of the network of architectonic signs, as well as their systemic correlates in the hierarchical network of linguistic signs. What is presented below is a provisional sketch of such relationships seen by the writer as this book goes to press. Moreover, it should be borne in mind that the following chart is in part an artifact of the printed text: the relationships portrayed exist as figures in a complexly-multidimensional conceptual space. The 'levels' sketched represent in fact different *perspectives* on semiotic formation, and their edges are not as hard and fast as the diagram might suggest. The diagram attempts to portray the set of invariant *relationships* among entities in the code which have characteristic systemic functions, rather than a set of *objects*. Clearly, an architectonic *figure* in no way resembles a linguistic 'morpheme': but a *figure* bears a correlative relationship to other sign types in its code in the same systemic manner that a linguistic morpheme does in its. It is this nexus of relationships which the diagram below attempts, clumsily, to portray. The signs in any given code are a function of the systemic properties of the code as a whole: a code is not built up of signs any more than a house is built of bricks.

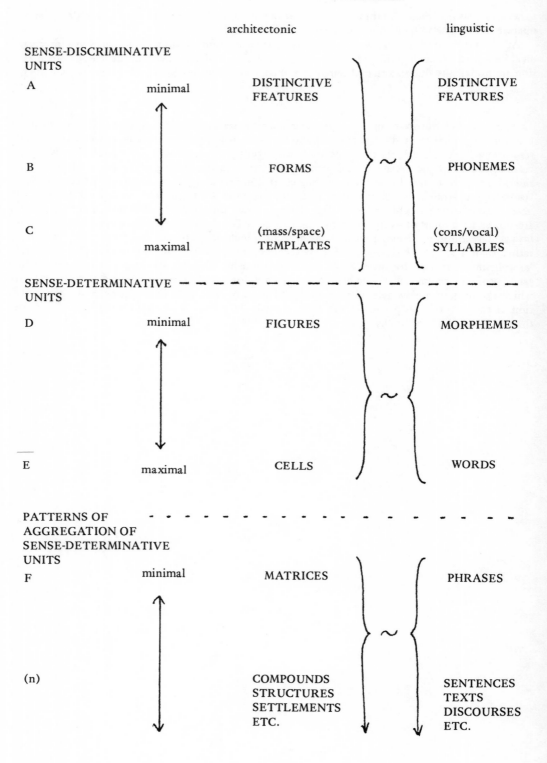

KEY TO DIAGRAM

A: Minimal sense-discriminative units, encoded as paradigmatic binary oppositions

B: Encoded as syntagmatically-simultaneous clusters of (A)

C: Maximal sense-discriminative units, encoded as syntagmatically-sequential arrays of (B), patterned alternations of (B) manifesting mass (consonantal) and space (vocalic) distinctive features

D: Minimal sense-determinative units, comprising one or more of (A), (B), or (C), either singly, simultaneously, or sequentially

E: Maximal sense-determinative units encoded as such in a system, comprising one or more of (D)

F: Minimal patterns of aggregation of sense-determinative units, comprising one or more of (E)

n: Maximal patterns of aggregation, comprising one or more of (F)

NOTE: the 'boundary' between sense-determinative units and patterns of aggregation of sense-determinative units is soft, and there may be considerable overlap between codal entities (E) and (F) in particular codes and contexts.

Glossary

Some of the terminology used in this study may be new or unfamiliar to the reader, and some of it consists of terms used in a technical fashion. The following glossary is intended as a guide to these usages. Terms are indexed to the text by page numbers to their first occurrence and in some cases to text explanations and definitions. In the text, the first occurrence of a special term is noted by a superscript letter (thus, aesthetic[a]).

AESTHETIC (64): see FUNCTION.

ARCHITECTONIC (1): pertaining to the formative organization of built environments (inclusive of architectural formations as well as formations appropriated semiotically (qv) from given natural landscapes).

ARCHITECTONICS (3): the systematic study and analysis of architectonic formations.

ARTIFACTUAL (1, 5): pertaining to objects or formations made by human means (in contrast to formations designated or appropriated from a given landscape).

BUILT ENVIRONMENT (1): the ordered array of architectonic formations in a given environmental setting, both artifactual and appropriated.

CELL (38): see SPACE-CELL.

CHANNEL (5): sensory channel (e.g., vision, audition, olfaction); see MODALITY.

CODE (1): the system (qv) of ordered relationships and rules governing the relationships among significant formations.

COMMUNICATIVE EVENT (3): the totality of formations in the transmission of a message, involving units drawn from a variety of media, addressed to several sensory channels simultaneously: see MULTIMODAL.

COMPOSITION (76, 78): an ordered relationship among formations.

CONJUNCTION (83): an additive relationship among formations.

CONTEXTUAL VARIATION (43): differential manifestations of the same formation in contrastive situations or contexts of other formations: see RELATIONAL INVARIANCE.

CORRELATIVITY (68, 69): relationships which are similar in a systemic sense (qv) in different systems or codes.

DISJUNCTION (83): alternative realization or manifestation; an either-or relationship.

EMOTIVE (67): see FUNCTION.

EXPRESSIVE (67): see FUNCTION.

FORM (46): a subcellular unit in a geometric framework which is primarily significant in discriminating cellular units.

FORMAL STRUCTURE (62): the geometric, perspectival and topological set of organizational rules in a code; contrast material structure (qv).

FEATURES (50): the simultaneous set of spatial properties which serve to define subcellular units such as forms.

FUNCTION (63): the relationships among various components of a transmission; differently dominant orientations on these components prescribe contrastive functions (aesthetic, emotive, expressive, referential, meta-architectonic, territorial or phatic). See detailed explication, Chapter IV.

ICONIC (71): a relationship among signs wherein a formation purports to resemble its referent in varying degrees, from representational to diagrammatic.

INDEXICAL (71): a relationship among signs wherein a formation conjures up its referent via immediate contiguity.

INFRASTRUCTURE (5): the set of formations which subdivide a space-cell, such as furniture, etc., of a static or movable nature.

MATRIX (39): a sign formation comprising a diagram of syntactic relationship among space-cells; the pattern of aggregation of cells.

MATERIAL STRUCTURE (62): the set of organizational rules defining the composition of physical entities employed in the realization of architectonic sign-formations.

META-ARCHITECTONIC (65): see FUNCTION.

MODALITY (6): a code or system addressed to a given sensory channel.

MODULARITY (78): a set of ordered rules defining the patterned size-relationships of material composition.

MULTIFUNCTIONALITY (4, 63): a property of architectonic sign-formations wherein each transmission reveals the copresence of various functions (qv).

MULTIMODALITY (3): a property of communicative events (qv) wherein the totality of the message is addressed simultaneously to several sensory channels and different semiotic codes.

PHATIC (65): see TERRITORIALITY: FUNCTION.

PLANES (52): a subcellular systemic unit in a two-dimensional space frame whose significance involves a portion of the definition and discrimination of cells.

POLYSEMOUS (66): multiply-meaningful.

PRESCRIPTIVE (4): pertaining to theory in *applied* architectonics (architectural practice), in contrast to descriptive theory, having to do with the analysis of architectonic systems *per se*.

REFERENTIALITY (64): a functional orientation upon the contextual associations or usages of a formation (see FUNCTION).

RELATIONAL INVARIANCE (2): invariance or constancy across sets of different realizations of formation.

SEMATECTONIC (43, 63): pertaining to direct signification of any architectonic formation; applies to systemic as well as directly-meaningful units or formations in a code.

SEMIOTIC (1): pertaining to significance or meaningfulness of sign-formations in any kind of communicative system. A code is a semiotic system or system of signs.

SEMIOTIC CONSTRAINT (47): sets of rules proscribing the conventional occurrence of certain sign-formations; regulations on what a corpus of formations considers as non-proper in some sense.

SENSE-DETERMINATIVE (50): pertaining to forms and features which have direct (as well as systemic) significance, to be contrasted with sense-discriminative or systemic meaningfulness.

SIGN (2): a combination of a formation or that-which-signifies and a referent, or that-which-is-signified. I.e., both a formation *and* its conceptual association(s).

SIGNANS (70): the formative component of a sign: that which signifies.

SIGNATUM (70): the associative component of a sign: that which is signified.

SIGN SYSTEM (3): see CODE.

SINGULARITY OF DENOTATION (50): sense-determinative meaning (qv).

SOMATOTOPY (6, 49): significant spatial behavior wherein formations created by differential orientations and movements of body-parts are incorporated into systems or codes of somatic signs: cf. kinesics, proxemics, body language, etc.

SPACE-CELL (38): the primary significant unit in an architectonic code, comprising an alterna-pattern of mass and space components (forms, planes). Includes both enclosed spaces and objects plus their surrounds.

SPACE-MANIFOLD (50): a spatial framework, of three types in an architectonic system—geo-metric, perspectival and topological.

STRING (60): a network of connections among space-cells; the geometric pattern of matrices.

SYMBOLIC (71): a relationship among signs wherein the formation is tied to its associated refer-ent in a conventional and arbitrary fashion (i.e., without iconicity or indexicality.

SYSTEM (1): see CODE.

SYSTEMATICITY (4): the orderliness of a code; its internal organization.

SYSTEMIC (2): pertaining to the structure and organization of a code and its component unities. Thus, subcellular units are significant in a systemic way primarily, in contrast to cellular units, which carry direct extra-systemic associations.

TERRITORIALITY (65): see FUNCTION.

* * * *

The following symbols are employed in the text on a couple of occasions as a graphic shorthand:

$>$ (40) = "greater than" ($>>$ = very much greater than)

$<$ (40) = "lesser than" ($<<$ = very much lesser than)

(80) = ($c = a$ and b)

(80) = ($c = a$ or b)

Bibliography

The following list includes all sources and references in the text, as well as books and articles which in various ways have influenced the present study. The bibliography is also intended to serve as an introductory guide to the subject of the study of the built environment.

The items below are numbered consecutively. Some of these consist of important artices published in collections and anthologies; these are cross-indexed by number.

The listing includes writings on architectural theory, semiotics, nonverbal communication, and anthropology, as well as works on the subject of Minoan architecture and culture for those wishing to pursue more detailed study of the data employed in our analytic corpus. Many of the following works are particularly useful for their extensive bibliographies (indicated by an asterisk). An especially useful introduction to semiotics and structuralism is Hawkes (*34*), and the most important introduction to the study of the phonological structure of verbal language is Jakobson and Waugh (*45*), for those interested in a comparative look at non-architectonic communication. The best sources of bibliography for nonverbal communication in general are M. R. Key, items *49* and *50*.

1. AGREST, D., and GANDELSONAS, M. "Semiotics and the Limits of Architecture," in *118*, 90-120.
2. ALEXANDER, C. *Notes on the Synthesis of Form* (Cambridge, MA, 1964).
3. ARNHEIM, R. *Toward a Psychology of Art* (Berkeley, 1966).
4. —————— *Visual Thinking* (New York, 1971).
5. BACHELARD, G. *The Poetics of Space* (Boston, 1970).
6. BASSO, K., and SELBY, H., eds. *Meaning in Anthropology* (Albuquerque, New Mexico, 1976).
7. BENTHALL, J., ed. *The Limits of Human Nature* (New York, 1974).
8. BERGER, P., and LUCKMANN, T. *The Social Construction of Reality* (New York, 1966).
9. BURNETTE, C. M. "Toward a Technical Theory of Architectural Design," in *Man-Environment Systems*, July 1969.
10. CASSIRER, E. *The Philosophy of Symbolic Forms* (I) (New Haven, 1968).
11. CHANG, K. C. *Rethinking Archaeology* (New York, 1967).
12. —————— *Settlement Archaeology* (New York, 1970).
13. CHARBONNIER, G. *Conversations with Claude Levi-Strauss* (London, 1969).
14. CICOUREL, A. V. *Cognitive Sociology* (London, 1973).
15. COLLINS, P. *Changing Ideals in Modern Architecture* (London, 1965).
16. COUSIN, J. *Topological Organization of Architectural Spaces* (Montreal, 1970).

17. DAVENPORT, W. "Marshallese Islands Navigational Charts," in *Imago Mundi* XV, 1960, 19-26.

18. DE GEORGE, R. and F., eds. *The Structuralists from Marx to Levi-Strauss* (New York, 1972).

19. DE LONG, A. Review of Hall, E. T., The Hidden Dimension, in *Man-Environment Systems*, September 1972.

20. _____. "The Communication Process: a Generic Model for Man-Environment Relations," in *Man-Environment Systems*, September 1972.

21. DOWNS, R. M., and STEA, D., eds. *Cognitive Mapping: Images of Spatial Development* (New York, 1971).

*22. ECO, U. *A Theory of Semiotics* (Bloomington, Indiana, 1976).

*23. *EDRA III*: Proceedings of the 3rd Environmental Design Research Conference, Los Angeles, January 1972, ed. W. J. Mitchell.

24. FATOURIS, D. A. "The Perceptual Organization of the Work of Architecture," in *Man-Environment Systems*, September 1971.

25. FAIRSERVIS, W. A. *The Threshold of Civilization* (New York, 1975).

26. FOUCAULT, M. *The Order of Things* (New York, 1970).

27. _____ *The Archaeology of Knowledge* (New York, 1972).

28. GOLDIN-MEADOW, S., and FELDMAN, H. "The Development of Language-Like Communication without a Language Model," *Science*, Vol. 197, 401-3, 22 July 1977.

29. GOMBRICH, E. N., HOCHBERG, J., and BLACK, M. *Art, Perception and Reality* (London, 1972).

30. GOODNOW, J. *Children Drawing* (Cambridge, MA, 1977).

31. GOULD, S. J. "The Shape of Things to Come," in *Systematic Zoology*, 22.4, December 1973, 401-404.

32. _____ "D'Arcy Thompson and the Science of Form," in *New Literary History* 1973, 229-258.

33. HART, R. D., and MOORE, G. T. "The Development of Spatial Cognition," in *23*.

*34. HAWKES, T. *Structuralism & Semiotics* (Berkeley, 1977).

35. HAYNES, R. "Behavior Space & Perceptor Space: a Reconnaissance," in *Man-Environment Systems*, July 1970.

36. HERSCHENBERGER, R. "Toward a Set of Semantic Scales to Measure the Meaning of Architectural Events," in *23*, section 6.4.1.

37. HILLIER, MUSGROVE & O'SULLIVAN, "Knowledge & Design," in *23*, section 29.3.1.

38. HOCHBERG, J. "The Representation of Things & People," in *29*, 47-94.

39. HOGG, J., ed. *Physchology & the Visual Arts* (London, 1969).

40. HONIKIAN, B. "An Investigation of the Relationship Between Construing the Environment and its Physical Form," in *23*, 6.5.1.

41. HYMES, D. *Linguistic Models in Archaeology* (mimeograph, 1969).

42. _____. *Reinventing Anthropology* (New York, 1974).

43. _____. *Foundations in Sociolinguistics* (Philadelphia, 1974).

44. JAKOBSON, R. *Coup d'Oeil sur le Developpement de la Semiotique* (Bloomington, Ind., 1975).

*45. _____, and WAUGH, L. *The Sound Shape of Language* (Bloomington, Ind., 1979).

46. JENCKS, C. *Meaning in Architecture* (New York, 1970).

47. KAPLAN, R. "The Dimensions of the Visual Environment: Methodological Considerations," in *23*, section 6.7.1.

48. KAPLAN, S. "Adaptation, Structure & Knowledge: a Biological Perspective," in *23*, section 30.6.1.

*49. KEY, M. R. *Paralanguage and Kinesics (Nonverbal Communication) with a Bibliography* (1975).

50. _____. Nonverbal Communication: a Research Guide and Bibliography (1977).

51. KAUFMANN-DIAMMAT, S. "Some Requirements for a Theory of Environmental Cognition: an Information-Processing View," in *23*, 30.7.1.

52. KUBLER, G. *The Shape of Time* (New Haven, 1965).

53. LANCASTER, J. B. *Primate Behavior and the Emergence of Human Culture* (New York, 1975).

54. LEACH, E. B. *Culture and Communication* (New York, 1975).

55. LE CORBUSIER. *Maniere de penser l'urbanisme* (Paris, 1966).

56. LEVIN, H. *Why Literary Criticism is not an Exact Science* (Cambridge, MA, 1967).

57. LEVI-STRAUSS, C. *Totemism* (Boston, 1963).

58. _____. *Tristes Tropique* (New York, 1965).

59. _____. *The Savage Mind* (Chicago, 1966).

60. _____. *The Scope of Anthropology* (London, 1967).

61. _____. *The Raw and the Cooked* (New York, 1969).

62. LORRAIN, F. *Reseaux sociaux et classifications sociales* (Paris, 1975).

63. LYNCH, K. *The Image of the City* (Cambridge, MA, 1960).

64. _____. *What Time is this Place?* (Cambridge, MA, 1975).

65. MARCUS, C. C. "The House as Symbol of Self," *Designing for Human Behavior* 1974, 130-146.

66. MARSHACK, A. *The Roots of Civilization* (New York, 1972).

67. MARSHALL, L. "!Kung Bushman Bands," *Africa* 30.4., 1960, 342-343.

68. MAUDET, C. *Methodes scientifiques, modeles et simulation en architecture* (Paris, 1973).

69. MERLEAU-PONTY, M. *Signs* (Chicago, 1964).

70. _____. *The Structure of Behavior* (Boston, 1963).

71. MITCHELL, W., ed. *EDRA III* (see above, item *23*).

72. MOLES, A. *Information Theory & Aesthetic Perception* (Chicago, 1966).

73. MOORE, G. T. "Conceptual Issues in the Study of Environmental Cognition," in *23*, section 29.3.1.

74. _____ . "Elements of a Genetic-Structural Theory of Environmental Cognition," in *23*, section 30.9.1.

75. MOORE, M. K. "Object Permanence and Object Identity: a Stage Developmental Model," (paper presented to the Society for Research in Child Development, Denver, 1975).

76. MORRIS, D. *Signification and Significance* (Cambridge, MA, 1964).

77. MOYNIHAN, M. *The New World Primates: Adaptive Radiation and the Evolution of Social Behavior, Languages and Intelligence* (Princeton, NJ, 1977).

78. MUKAŘOVSKÝ, J. *Structure, Sign and Function: Selected Writings* (New Haven, 1978).

79. NEGROPONTE, N. *The Architecture Machine* (Cambridge, MA, 1970).

80. NEISSER, U. *Cognition and Reality* (San Francisco, 1976).

81. NEWMAN, R. J. "The Basis of Architectural Design: Intuition or Research?" in *Oxford Architectural Research Papers*, I, December 1974, Oxford, England.

82. NODELMAN, S. "Some Remarks on Structural Analysis in Art," in *Yale French Studies* 36-37, 1966, 89-102, New Haven, CT.

*83. NORBERG-SCHULZ, C. *Intentions in Architecture* (Cambridge, MA, 1965).

84. _____. *Existence, Space and Architecture* (New York, 1971).

*85. PANOFSKY, I. *Studies in Iconology* (New York, 1962).

86. PEIRCE, C. S. *Collected Writings* (Cambridge, MA, 1921-1948).

87. PIAGET, J. *The Origins of Intelligence in Children* (New York, 1963).

88. _____. *The Child's Conception of Time* (New York, 1969).

89. _____. *Genetic Epistemology* (New York, 1970).

90. _____. *Structuralism* (New York, 1970).

91. _____. *Insights and Illusions of Philosophy* (New York and Cleveland, 1971).

92.   _____. *Biology and Knowledge* (Chicago, 1971).
93.   _____. *Main Trends in Interdisciplinary Research* (New York, 1973).
94.   _____, and INHELDER, B. *The Child's Conception of Space* (New York, 1967).
95.   PREZIOSI, D. "An Introduction to Functional Analysis in Architecture," in *Labrys* I. 1., March 1970, New Haven, CT.
96.   _____. "A Model for Architectural Design," in *Urban Studies Bulletin*, VIII, 1970, 1-5.
97.   _____. "Modular Design in Minoan Architecture," in *Studies Presented to G. M. A. Hanfmann* (Cambridge, MA, 1971).
98.   _____. "The Non-dichotomy of Sensory and Grammatical Relations," in *LACUS II*, 1976.
99.   _____. "Toward a Relational Theory of Culture," in *LACUS III, 1977.*
100.   _____. "Relations Between Environmental and Linguistic Structure," in Proceedings of the Wenner-Gren Foundation Symposium on the Semiotics of Language and Culture, Burg-Wartenstein, Austria, 1975 (to appear).
101.   _____. "Language and Perception," in *LACUS IV*, 1978 (1978a).
102.   _____. *Linguistic and Architectonic Signs* (1978b) (The Hague, forthcoming).
*103. _____. *The Origins of the Built World* (1978c) (The Hague, forthcoming).
104.   _____. "Architectonic and Linguistic Signs," paper presented to the International Conference on the Semiotics of Art, Ann Arbor, Michigan, May 3, 1978 (to be published) (1978d).
105.   _____. "Multimodal Communication" (1978k).
106.   _____. "The Parameters of the Architectonic Code" (1978f).
*107. PROSHANSKY, H. M., ITTLESON, W. H. and RIVLIN, L., eds. *Environmental Psychology* (New York, 1970).
108.   PYE, D. *The Nature of Design* (New York and London, 1964).
109.   RAND, G. "Children's Images of Houses," in *23*, section 6.9.1.
*110. RAPOPORT, Amos. *House Form and Culture* (Englewood Cliffs, NJ, 1969).
111.   _____. "Observations Regarding Man-Environment Studies," in *Man-Environment Systems*, January 1970.
112.   _____. "Australian Aborigines and the Definition of Place," in *23*, section 3.3.1.
113.   RYKWERT, J. *Adam's House in Paradise* (London, 1976).
114.   SCOTT, A. *Combinatorial Programming, Spatial Analysis and Planning* (London, 1971).
*115. SEBEOK, T. A. "Animal Communication," in *Science* CXLVII, 1965, 1006 ff.
*116. _____. *Perspectives in Zoosemiotics* (The Hague and Paris, 1972).
*117. _____. *Contributions to the Doctrine of Signs* (Bloomington, Ind., 1976).
118.   _____. *A Perfusion of Signs* (ed.) (Bloomington, Ind., 1977).
*119. SIEGMAN, A., and FELDSTEIN, S., eds. *Nonverbal Behavior and Communication* (New York, 1978).
120.   SIEGMAN, A., and POPE, B. *Studies in Dyadic Communication* (New York, 1972).
121.   SILVERSTEIN, M. "Shifters, Linguistic Categories and Cultural Description," in *6*, 11-56.
122.   SOMMER, R. *Personal Space: the Behavioral Basis of Design* (Englewood Cliffs, 1969).
123.   _____. "Studies in Personal Space," in *Sociometry* 22, 1959, 247-262.
124.   SPERBER, D. *Rethinking Symbolism* (Cambridge, Eng., 1975).
125.   SUMMERSON, J. *The Classical Language of Architecture* (Cambridge, MA, 1963).
126.   TEICH, M. and YOUNG, R., eds. *Perspectives in the History of Science: Essays in Honor of Joseph Needham* (New York, 1972).
127.   THOMPSON, D'A. *On Growth and Form* (Cambridge, Eng., 1971: abridged reissue).
128.   TZONIS, A., FREEMAN, M., LEFAIVRE, L., SALAMA, O., BERWICK, R., DE COINTET, E. *Systèmes conceptuels, de l'architecture en France de 1650 à 1800* (C.O.R.D.A., 1975).

129. VENTURI, R. *Complexity and Contradiction in Architecture* (New York, 1966).
130. VITRUVIUS. *The Ten Books on Architecture* (New York, 1960); translation of M. H. Morgan, 1914.
131. VON FRISCH, K. *Animal Architecture* (New York, 1974).
132. WALLIS, M. "Semantic and Symbolic Elements in Architecture: Iconology as a First Step Towards an Architectural Semiotic," in *Semiotica* 8:3 (1973) 220-238.
133. _____. *Arts and Signs* (Bloomington, Ind., 1975).
134. WATHEN-DUNN, W., ed. *Models for the Perception of Speech and Visual Form* (Cambridge, MA, 1967).
135. WHORF, B. L. *Language, Thought and Reality* (Cambridge, MA, 1956).
*136. WILSON, E. O. *Sociobiology: the New Synthesis* (Cambridge, MA, 1975), Section on Communication only.
137. WITHERSPOON, G. *The Central Concepts of Narajo World View* (Lisse, Holland, 1975).
138. YELLEN, J. *Archaeological Approaches to the Present: Models for Reconstructing the Past* (New York, 1977).

MINOAN ARCHITECTURE AND ARCHAEOLOGY

The bibliography pertaining to Minoan settlements is extensive, and the following is intended as a brief guide to major reports and surveys. The most useful introduction to Minoan architecture remains Graham's *Palaces of Crete*, wherein will also be found a good list of major excavation reports of primary sites:

*139. GRAHAM, J. W. *The Palaces of Crete* (Princeton, 1962).

See also the same author's:

140. _____ . "The Minoan Unit of Length and Minoan Palace Planning," in *American Journal of Archaeology* 64, 1960, 335-341.

For a contrary view on the planning methods of Minoan builders, see:

141. PREZIOSI, D. *Minoan Palace Planning and its Origins* (1968), unpublished Ph.D. dissertation, Harvard University.
142. _____ . "Modular Design in Minoan Architecture: an Introduction," in *Studies Presented to G. M. A. Hanfmann*, D. G. Mitten, J. G. Pedley, and J. A. Scott, eds., Cambridge, MA, 1971, 127-143.

The best general introductions to the Minoan civilization are:

*143. EVANS, A. J. *The Palace of Minos at Knossos*, vols. I-IV (London, 1921-1936).
144. MARINATOS, S., and HIRMER, M. *Crete and Mycenae* (New York, 1960).
145. MATZ, F. *Kreta, Mykene, Troia* (Stuttgart, 1957).
146. PENDLEBURY, J. D. S. *The Archaeology of Crete* (London, 1936).
147. PERNIER, G. *Il Palazzo Minoico di Festos* I (Roma, 1935).
148. _____ and BANTI, L. *Il Palazzo Minoico di Festos II* (Roma, 1951).

References to specific sites mentioned in the text, including Mallia, Tylissos, Rousses, Tou Vrakhnous O Lakkos, Knossos, will be found in *139* above. All of the general references cited above include extensive bibliographies. Additional discussion of Minoan architecture may be found in

149.   PREZIOSI, D. *142.*
150.   _____ . "Minoan Architectural Planning Methods," in *American Journal of Archaeology*, March 1967: conference report.
151.   _____ . "Harmonic Design in Ancient Architecture," *American Journal of Archaeology*, March 1968, conference report.
152.   _____ . "Modular Planning in Ancient Design," in *Fibonacci Quarterly*: Journal of Mathematics of the University of California VIII, April 1968.
153.   _____ . "The Conceptual Organization of the Egyptian House," in *American Journal of Archaeology*, April 1971, conference report.

Preliminary reports on the architectonic analysis of Minoan and other material appeared in three mimeographed monographs prepared at MIT for the writer's graduate seminars in architectonic analysis and theory:

154.   PREZIOSI, D. "Architecture and Cognition" (1974).
155.   _____ . "Dynamic Equivalence" (1974).
156.   _____ . "Architecture, Language and Meaning" (1975).